MANAGING PSYCHOSIS:
An Australian Guide

MANAGING PSYCHOSIS:
An Australian Guide

MARK TAYAR
&
MARGARET TAYAR

Rev. date: 04/12/2019

To order additional copies of this book, contact:
Xlibris
1-800-455-039
www.Xlibris.com.au
Orders@Xlibris.com.au
782347

Acknowledgements

Thank you to the contributors to vignettes in this book. Also, thank you to SANE Australia, who, through the Hocking Fellowship, funded the interviews that led to Jamie's vignettes.

Image Credits

Images belong to wewewegrafikbaydeh, paulbr75, Geralt, avi_acl and ISSUES on Pixabay as well as rawpixel.com on Pexels.

Word cloud generated from WordClouds.com from word frequency in this book.

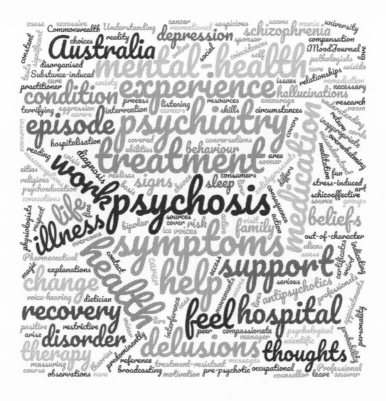

Contents

Introduction to the guide

Psychosis is a complex mental health condition where the person has difficulty distinguishing what is real from what is imagined. The person may hear, see, feel and believe things that are real in their own head but aren't actually happening. This is confusing and frightening and may be dangerous to themselves or others if they act on their false realities. According to the Australian Department of Health, 45 per cent of the population will experience a mental illness of some kind – such as depression, anxiety, or stress – over their lifetime. Within a twelve-month period, about 'one in every two hundred adult Australians will experience a psychotic illness' (SANE Australia). It is important to remember that psychosis is an illness and that it is treatable.

There is an increasing focus on raising awareness, diagnosis, treatment and support for people with mental health conditions. However, the focus has not extended to the more severe end of the mental health conditions – that is, to the complex mental health conditions such as schizophrenia and bipolar disorders that frequently include psychotic episodes. Complex mental health conditions have limited treatment options, poor coordination of services and relatively few resources to support treatment and recovery, even though their very complexity makes it difficult to negotiate the journey through a psychotic episode, the life-changing aftermath and living with a complex mental illness for a period or sometimes for your whole life.

Not only are there inadequate and fragmented treatment options, but also, people with complex mental health conditions experience discrimination and stigma in part because of ignorance, inadequate treatment and associated poor health outcomes.

Jack Heath, the dynamic CEO of SANE Australia, expresses the issues around complex mental illnesses succinctly:

> Now more than ever, people are seeking help for diagnoses such as depression and anxiety, but Australians living with complex mental health conditions still experience unacceptable levels of stigma and discrimination as well as poorer health and social and economic outcomes such as poverty, homelessness and unemployment.

This guide has been written for precisely these reasons – to address ignorance and inadequate treatment by helping people with symptoms of psychosis and their supporters negotiate their way through the maze that is mental health services to attain the best possible outcomes. The guide broadens recovery, encouraging people with psychosis to take an active role in recovery, focusing on building/rebuilding a healthy pattern of life with physical and psychological wellness, a strong support group, a network of friends and a rewarding array of activities to lead a full and productive life.

The guide focuses on providing a practical resource for people experiencing psychosis and their support persons. It is also hoped that the guide will start more conversations about psychosis and lead to greater awareness and more consumer-centred care.

The guide comes out of the lived experience of complex mental illnesses – negotiating through psychotic episodes, letting go of the old and understanding and accepting different sets of circumstances. It also comes out of the lived experience of building a life again in a new order – adjusting to new realities, renegotiating relationships, building personal and social relationships and starting from scratch again with work and a career. The guide also comes with the perspective of a carer, and as carers and consumers, we structure our experiences to research the literature and learn from it and apply it in a practical way to help those on a similar journey.

The guide is structured around the pathway through psychosis to resuming a full and productive life, keeping symptoms in check and avoiding recurrences. The steps in the pathway are the following:

- Understanding psychosis
- Early identification and minimising harm
- Managing a psychotic episode
- Recovery and renewal

This guide is as much for support people as it is for people experiencing psychotic episodes. The role of supporter will be both rewarding and challenging. Supporting people through psychotic episodes is particularly challenging as the person you are supporting may, at times, be out of touch with reality and not their normal selves. They may at times be living through terrifying experiences in the form of hallucinations and delusions. They may, at times, treat support persons disrespectfully. Support persons may, at times, need to make difficult decisions to get them professional help without their consent. Through all this, it is important to remember that they have an illness. The illness can be treated, and they will improve. You need to listen and remain calm. You need your own support mechanisms.

Mental health is not merely the absence of disease. Achieving 'mental health' involves actively working on all aspects of your life throughout your life to achieve a healthy and fulfilling life. Every journey is different. We hope this guide helps you with your journey.

Understanding psychosis

A brief history of psychosis

The word *psychosis* is of Greek origin, combining the words *psyche*, meaning soul or mind, and *osis*, meaning a diseased condition. There is evidence that people have experienced psychosis for millennia. In some ancient cultures, people with symptoms were recognised as shamans, mediums and prophets, while in others, they've been seen as possessed by demons.

History records many famous people who have experienced symptoms of psychosis at some stages of their lives but have also made valuable contributions to their communities. Famous people who have reportedly experienced psychosis have come from all walks of life, including ancient philosopher Socrates, French heroine Joan of Arc, artist Vincent Van Gogh, Eduard Einstein, son of Albert Einstein, writer Charles Dickens, poet William Blake, Indian activist Mahatma Gandhi, the founder of psychoanalysis, Sigmund Freud, Nobel Prize winner John Nash, Peter Green from Fleetwood Mac, actors Carrie Fisher and Anthony Hopkins, rapper Ol' Dirty Bastard, Jonathan Van Ness from *Queer Eye* and Mexican American musician Carlos Santana. All were reported to have experienced psychosis at some stage of their lives.

You are not alone if you have experienced symptoms of psychosis. You may be labelled as different and treated in a stigmatised way. You can make valuable contributions to your communities. We are at least fortunate today to have a variety of different treatment options to help combat psychosis.

Definition of psychosis

In its simplest form, psychosis may be defined as conditions that affect the mind where there has been some loss of contact with reality (National

Institute of Mental Health, USA). Psychosis is not strictly a 'disease' in its own right. It is a situation where the person exhibits symptoms that are out of touch with reality. Symptoms of psychosis may manifest in a number of mental health conditions.

Symptoms of psychosis

Common symptoms of psychosis

Common symptoms of psychosis include the following:

- Confused thinking such as forgetting things, difficulty concentrating and following conversations
- Seeing, hearing, feeling, smelling and tasting things that aren't real (hallucinations), such as hearing voices
- Beliefs that aren't real (delusions), like believing that people around you are spying on you
- Changed feelings such as the absence of emotions or mood swings between happiness and depression for no apparent reason
- Changed behaviours such as the inability to do anything or, conversely, excessive activity at any time of the day or night
- Inappropriate behaviours such as laughing or crying for no apparent reason, irritability or aggression

Other symptoms

Psychosis is a more serious mental health condition because it is characterised by difficulty distinguishing between what is real and what is not. As a consequence, you may have difficulty interpreting whether things are actually happening to you or you are imagining them. This can, for example, be dangerous if you act on these false beliefs. It is therefore important for you to be particularly alert to any changes in yourself that you feel are uncharacteristic of you or 'strange'.

Symptoms of psychosis to look out for and that entail appropriate action include the following:

- **Feelings**
  - Feeling that no one understands you
  - Thinking that people are talking about you
  - Sensing that you are disconnected from the world
  - Feeling like your senses are sharper or feeling new sensations
  - Becoming paranoid about being monitored or watched
  - Noticing a series of unusual coincidences
  - Repeated epiphanies, like you have realised something incredible

- **Disorganised speech**, which is usually a reflection of disorganised thoughts and may involve constantly switching topics or jumbling up words

- **Abnormal behaviour**, which may manifest in a variety of forms, such as acting like a child, swearing out loud without reason or catatonic behaviour, where there is a complete lack of movement or uncontrollable excessive movement

- **'Negative symptoms'**, which may also manifest in a variety of forms, including decreased emotional expression, less motivation to do activities like work or socialising, less speaking and decreased ability to get pleasure from activities that are usually pleasurable

- **Sense of passivity**, such as feeling your thoughts don't belong to you (This may be accompanied with a delusion that some other being or electronic device put thoughts in your head. Remember that this sort of delusion is common to those experiencing psychosis and is not real. Thought broadcasting, where you feel that others can hear your thoughts, may also occur. Thought withdrawal, where you feel thoughts are being taken from your head, is another passivity experience.)

In the early stages of psychosis, you may be able to recognise the changes as 'strange', but delusions mean you believe your imaginings are real despite logic and evidence. You may have no insight into the seriousness of your condition. Even at the time of diagnosis of psychosis, up to 50–80 per cent of people with first-episode psychosis have poor insight into having a mental illness (Tordesillas-Gutierrez et al, 2018). This means that it is essential to have support people around you who are also aware of early warning signs and that you are open with them about possible symptoms, listen to their feedback, don't ignore evidence that contradicts the delusion and seek help if they confirm your fears.

Lack of insight into deteriorating symptoms of psychosis places an added responsibility on family and friends who may notice changes in the person they love. They may try to discuss these changes with the person. Their feedback may be ignored or argued against as the person believes in the delusion, and questioning it may lead to aggressive responses (such as paranoia), which may be part of the illness. This situation is particularly difficult as the person with the symptoms may not believe they need help, and the family member or friend is placed in the position of needing to seek help for the person. This is difficult if the person refuses to seek help. It is also a worry to the support person because they don't want to jeopardise their relationship with their loved one.

Symptoms of psychosis that may be observed by others

As an observer or support person, you may become aware of changes in behaviour in someone you care about or are associated with. You can look for changes in what the person says and what they do. This includes the following:

What they say

- Slowed speech, unusual phrases or constant changing of topics
- Rapid speech and racing ideas
- Out-of-character references to spirituality or nature
- Obsession with being watched by cameras or people
- Intense preoccupation with one subject
- Saying they can't tune out street noise or other people talking in the distance

What they do

- Pacing or agitation
- Laughing at inappropriate times

- Poor personal hygiene that is out of character
- Desire to be alone
- Suspiciousness
- Being unresponsive to your questions
- Lack of sleep
- Extreme emotions or total lack of emotions
- Facial expressions and body language that shows emotions that are the opposite of what they are saying

Pay attention to any changes that you notice. Be particularly alert if you notice several of these changes and if they are getting worse or do not appear to be going away. Do not ignore them. Don't panic, but take action quickly.

As a trusted person, you can bring attention to changes and suggest that these may be a sign that professional help is needed. Remember that your goal is to get the person the help they need. Encourage them to go to a general practitioner (GP) or to a private clinic for those with private health insurance who can get through a waiting list quickly enough. If you are really worried, you can take them to the emergency department at your local hospital. You are doing the person a favour by helping them to take action as soon as you notice changes. This may avert a psychotic episode. Early intervention improves the outcomes.

Potentially dangerous symptoms of psychosis

Thoughts or feelings that require immediate medical professional help include the following:

- Thoughts of death or a plan to commit suicide
- Feeling like you are a burden on your friends and family
- Having a sense of extreme loneliness
- Feeling like you don't belong anywhere
- Voices in your head telling you to harm yourself or others

The most dangerous symptom of psychosis is the risk of harming yourself or harming others. Self-harming may take many forms, including having suicidal thoughts and/or a plan of how to kill yourself. It may also take less obvious forms, such as harm to your reputation, harm to relationships, harm to your financial position, the inability to take care of yourself or the potential for misadventure and relapse.

If you are thinking about suicide or harming yourself in any way, you need to seek immediate help by going to the emergency department in your local hospital, seeking admission to a psychiatric facility or phoning 000 and requesting an ambulance. If you have a family member who has attempted or committed suicide, you are at greater risk of suicidal thoughts and intentions. You are at even greater risk of suicide if you have a plan on how to do it. If you do have a plan, you need to seek professional help immediately and remove yourself from being able to act on that plan, especially if you think a psychotic episode is about to occur. It's important to remember that however bad you feel, medication and therapy can help you recover.

In some situations, such as having paranoid thoughts or feelings of persecution, you may feel that you want to harm other people. You may even put yourself in dangerous situations, such as confronting people you are paranoid about. If you have these thoughts or are feeling this way, you need to go to the emergency department of your local hospital or phone 000 and request an ambulance. This may lead to hospitalisation, which can be traumatising but is less traumatising than remaining psychotic.

It is also possible that in your confused state of mind, anxiety and fear of what is happening to you and feeling out of control, you may take it out on others. You may get irritable and angry with people around you. You may treat those who are trying to help you badly. It is important for you and your support persons to remember that this is not your normal behaviour, that you have an illness. However, it is also no excuse for poor behaviour. You need to seek treatment. Treatment will reduce your symptoms, anxiety and fears, help you get in touch with reality and help you to improve your behaviour.

Types of mental health disorders with psychotic features

Symptoms of psychosis occur in a number of different types of mental health disorders based on the nature of the symptoms. In the 1800s, psychiatrist Emil Kraepelin divided psychosis into two categories, which are now known as schizophrenia and bipolar. *Schizo* means split, but schizophrenia is not about split personalities but where the split between reality and fantasy becomes confused in your mind.

Today the two primary sources of psychiatric diagnosis – the *Diagnostic and Statistical Manual of Mental Disorders*, fifth edition (DSM-5), and the *International Classification of Diseases*, eleventh revision (ICD-11) – identify the different types of disorders that may include psychotic components. These are psychotic disorders, mood disorders, personality disorders and other disorders as detailed below.

Psychotic disorders

- Delusional disorder — delusion without hallucinations or only mild hallucinations related to a delusion
- Brief psychotic disorder — psychosis for at least a day but less than a month
- Schizophreniform disorder — psychosis for at least a month but less than six months
- Schizophrenia — probably the most feared of the psychotic disorders but exists on a spectrum and might not be severe but occurs for over six months

- Schizoaffective disorder — major depressive or manic episode as well as at least one period of psychosis that occurs without depression or mania
- Acute and transient psychotic disorder — psychosis without early warning signs, with the episode less than three months
- Substance-induced psychotic disorders — psychosis after intoxication or withdrawal
- Catatonic disorder — significantly decreased or excessive movement

Mood disorders with psychotic features

- Bipolar disorder — psychosis that may occur with mania (usually bipolar type I)
- Single-episode depressive disorder with psychotic symptoms
- Recurrent depressive disorder with psychotic symptoms
- Major depressive disorder with psychotic features

Personality disorders with psychotic features

- Schizotypal disorder — detachment from social relationships, less emotional expression and possible experience of brief psychotic episodes
- Borderline personality disorder (BPD) — about 20–50 per cent of people with BPD may experience psychosis (Schroeder, Fisher and Schäfer, 2013)

Other disorders that may have psychotic features in some cases

- Generalised anxiety disorder
- Panic disorder
- Autism
- Dementia
- Post-traumatic stress disorder (PTSD)
- Secondary psychotic syndrome (caused by a health condition other than mental or behavioural disorders)

- Mental or behavioural disorders associated with pregnancy, childbirth or the puerperium, with psychotic symptoms (especially postpartum psychosis)

Diagnoses of disorders that may include psychosis are made by psychiatrists. The diagnosis is based on the person's family and medical history, investigations and the type of symptoms experienced and how long they've had the symptoms. Medications are likely to be prescribed on the basis of the diagnosis. The diagnosis may change as symptoms change and/or during the course of the condition.

Factors and conditions that may increase the risk of psychosis

Factors that may increase the risk of psychosis

There isn't a single cause of psychosis. Psychosis is generally caused by a combination of factors that may either increase the risk of a psychotic episode or trigger an episode. These risk factors may include the following:

- Genetic predisposition (such as family history of psychosis)
- Biological factors (such as insomnia, dementia or other neurological conditions)
- Psychological factors (such as stress)
- Social factors (such as relationship problems)
- Environmental factors (such as isolation and childhood trauma)
- Life events (such as drug usage, the death of family a member and change events)

It is important to be aware of the factors that increase the risk of a psychotic episode. However, having these risk factors doesn't necessarily mean that you will have a psychotic episode. Many of these risk factors are a part of normal life. Life throws these challenges from time to time in your life. What is important is how you cope with these factors. Monitor your reactions and seek help if you are worried.

Research shows that only one-third of people who meet clinical high-risk criteria actually develop psychotic illness (Fusar-Poli, 2012). However, it is always easier to deal with symptoms and issues early. If you have any concerns, seek help. You may benefit from being able to talk through what is happening with a health professional, such as your GP or a psychologist. They can assess you, give you reassurance and allay your concerns, refer you to appropriate assistance, prescribe medication, support you to make lifestyle changes, direct you to therapy and generally assist you with early treatment to prevent symptoms from getting worse.

Lived experience vignette — Mark's risk factors

When I had my first major episode, I ticked many of the risk factors for psychosis. Still, I didn't know much about psychosis except from using psychedelic drugs and having a 'bad trip'. I have a genetic predisposition to bipolar but didn't really know much about this genetic risk. I believe that my first episode was primarily caused by work-related stress. I also had some insomnia leading up to the episode, which made dealing with continued stressors more difficult because of intense fatigue.

Supporter vignette — A mum's experience

People are not totally psychotic. They are only psychotic in some areas specific to them. These may be areas that are the essence of that person. Mark loves feeling like that again. I love seeing him like his old self. Where is the line in the sand? He is totally sane in some areas. He is smart. He is plausible. We want to believe he's OK. In our hearts, we know he's not. He is a little up, a little labile. He stays that way for a week. Then he tips over. We need to intervene early. I draw his attention to examples he is exhibiting from his emergency management plan, but he refutes them, says they are real issues that he hasn't resolved.

You need to know the early signs and symptoms. What are the particular symptoms that raise a red flag? Be alert to any changes. Are these the normal ups and downs of life, or is this a change that may escalate into something out of control? The shift may occur so quickly – a short glimpse of initiative, of the passion and excitement that was the essence of him. He is enjoying life. We are enjoying him getting a kick out of life – more like his old self. How far do you let it go? You hope he won't tip over into being out of control. You are alert, scared. His early signs include increase in activity, speeding up, doing lots of things at once, short attention span, inability to concentrate for any length of time and emotionally labile switching from highs to lows. Worst of all is the increasing criticism of those close to him, the growing paranoia that people are against him – what is real and what is imagined? Plausible in some areas, growing delusion in others – all the pain of past episodes bubbles up to the surface and spews out at those he holds responsible. He is past being able to reason with. You can draw attention to his emergency management plan, give him examples of the symptoms he's exhibiting, but his main symptoms are being critical and paranoid, so raising anything that can be deemed critical triggers a vicious attack on those he normally cares for. The problem then is how to get him the care he needs. He is a risk to himself. He is imagining that others are against him. When he does get admitted to hospital, he is in a very bad way. He is psychotic and paranoid. He does remember much of this later. He does understand how horrible he's been to those he loves. I guess he feels terrible about this. He has had a glimpse of his old self. He has been flying, as he used to do. He has been able to reduce his medication. How depressing all this is for him. I fear that he is suicidal.

Activity: Identifying and reducing risk factors of psychosis

List any risk factors for psychosis you feel you may have. Consider whether you feel you are coping adequately with these risk factors. If you have any concerns in any areas, outline the course of action you plan to take to reduce those risks.

Drug-induced psychosis

Drug-induced psychosis is a form of psychosis brought on by alcohol or other drug use or withdrawal from alcohol or drugs. Symptoms of psychosis may occur with alcohol, cannabis (including synthetic cannabis), opioids, hallucinogens, inhalants, sedatives, hypnotics, anti-anxieties, stimulants (including cocaine and ice) and other substances (DSM-5, 2013). The symptoms generally appear quickly. They may resolve quickly or last for longer periods. There is likely to be an increased risk of another episode if the substance is used again. The most common symptoms include visual hallucinations, disorientation and memory loss.

Even if you don't use drugs, it's important to know about drug-induced psychosis because sometimes hospital staff may think you have used drugs when you are present at hospital with symptoms of psychosis. In this case, it is important to request a drug test to confirm your condition is not drug related.

Psychosis occurs in about one in three people who regularly use ice (Bramness and Rognli, 2016). Approximately 30 per cent of people who experience ice psychosis develop a psychotic illness (Zarrabi et al, 2016). An early warning sign of potential psychosis with ice use is a pre-psychotic state where you believe that coincidences have a strong personal significance or a mood where you feel something ominous is coming on (Cadet and Gold, 2017). If you cease ice yourself or get treatment for ice addiction in this pre-psychotic state, you may be able to prevent an acute episode of psychosis.

Phone 000 and seek urgent medical assistance if you experience any unusual symptoms after alcohol or drug use. Early intervention and treatment may help alleviate a full-blown psychotic episode.

Substance abuse in psychosis

Using alcohol, cocktails of legal and/or prescribed medications and illicit drugs (including smoking) as a method of coping with psychosis is not recommended as they may interact with prescribed medications, worsen existing conditions and/or increase anxiety or cause depression. It is also possible to develop a dependence on drugs or alcohol, which may cause additional problems that require treatment. Mixing prescribed medications with alcohol or other drugs can also have dangerous consequences, including overdose and possibly death.

Changing habits is difficult, but eliminating the use of drugs and alcohol is something you can control to give yourself the best chance of making a full recovery from a psychotic episode. Remember to let your doctor know if you stop drinking alcohol or using drugs as this may affect the concentrations of medications in your blood. Your doctor may be able to reduce the doses of some of your medications.

Postnatal psychosis

Learning to manage a newly born child is hard enough without the complications of a psychotic episode. We are all aware of the so-called baby blues that women frequently experience after childbirth. Sleep deprivation and rapid hormonal changes after childbirth may be partly responsible for baby blues; however, it is important to be aware of uncharacteristic changes in behaviour or any signs of the new mother feeling out of touch with reality. In this case, seek immediate assessment by a medical practitioner – the earlier the treatment starts, the quicker the symptoms can be alleviated and a full-blown psychotic episode avoided.

Postnatal psychosis occurs after childbirth for one to two in one thousand mothers (PANDA, 2018). It usually occurs within the first four weeks of childbirth (Sit, Rothschild and Wisner, 2006). The illness is serious; however, it is treatable and generally resolved completely but may recur after subsequent pregnancies. Treatment generally involves medication and hospitalisation.

While the causes of postnatal psychosis are generally unknown, there are factors that increase the risk of a psychotic episode after childbirth. Women with bipolar disorder have an increased risk of a psychotic episode after childbirth. Women who have experienced a psychotic episode after a previous pregnancy may also have an increased risk of another psychotic episode.

Because the major feature of psychosis is being out of touch with reality, the mother with the symptoms may not be aware that she is imagining things. Her partner or other family member may be the ones who recognise the uncharacteristic behaviour. In this case, don't delay. Seek immediate medical help.

Hospitalisation is generally necessary to assess the condition, start medication and stabilise the condition. Medications require ongoing monitoring of the impact on the mother and the baby. Hospitalisation enables close monitoring of the medication while the mother stabilises. In the case of breastfeeding, it is important to discuss this with the specialist health professional as some particular medications (sodium valporate and clozapine) are not recommended, and others (such as lithium) should be used cautiously, and their impact on the mother and baby (if breastfeeding needs to be monitored closely) should be noted. Go to www.cope.org.au, the Centre of Perinatal Excellence website, for more information on the medication of postpartum psychosis.

Hospitalisation may be in a general adult hospital and your baby cared for at home or in a psychiatric mother–baby unit, where your baby will stay with you. It should be noted that there is currently only one mother–baby unit in Sydney and one in Melbourne.

Health professionals can provide a range of support to help address the needs of the mother. Support is also required to look after the baby and other family members whilst the mother is in hospital and after she returns home. It is important to remember that the condition is treatable and will resolve, and you will be able to return to your family and resume the care of your baby as your condition resolves.

An extensive support network is essential to achieve the best possible outcomes. Emotional and practical support is needed for the mother in hospital, the partner at home looking after the baby (if that is the case) and possibly other children in the family while the mother is hospitalised. Then there is the continuing support required when the mother is discharged from hospital and recovering and resuming the responsibilities associated with a newborn baby as well as the 'normal' responsibilities of a family.

Women with an increased risk of psychosis who plan to have other children need to seek specialist medical advice to prepare for the next pregnancy and the risk of another postnatal episode of psychosis. For example, women on mood stabilisers need to take folate supplements before they are pregnant and in the first trimester of pregnancy to reduce the small chance of increased birth defects associated with these medications. Women who've had previous episodes of psychosis should also have emergency management plans to help identify early signs of symptoms of psychosis and discuss management options etc. The plan should be shared with treating doctors and support persons.

For further information on postnatal psychosis, go to PANDA's (Perinatal Anxiety & Depression Australia) website, www.panda.org.au, or phone their national hotline (1300 726 306).

Psychosis in older people

With the sheer numbers and ageing of the baby boomers, there is likely to be a significant increase in the number of elderly people who suffer from mental illness. Psychosis can occur well into old age. Psychosis occurring for the first time in older people is generally due to conditions that often occur much later in life, such as dementia or neurologic conditions such as Parkinson's disease or stroke. Psychosis is common in Parkinson's disease, with over half of all people diagnosed with Parkinson's disease experiencing psychotic episodes (Forsaa et al, 2010).

Psychotic episodes or other neuropsychiatric episodes following a stroke occur in about 30 per cent of stroke survivors. Symptoms of psychosis after a stroke frequently have a delayed onset but may also be due to a subsequent 'silent stroke' ('Post-stroke psychosis: A systematic review', Stangeland et al, 2018). The review estimates that 'post-stroke psychosis affects approximately one in twenty patients with stroke in the post-acute stage, and . . . this may increase to approximately 7 per cent over subsequent years'.

Approximately 50 per cent of people with dementia experience symptoms of psychosis within the first three years of the diagnosis of dementia, although symptoms of psychosis are rarely the initial manifestation of dementia (Finkel, 2001). Common symptoms of psychosis in dementia that carers may notice are paranoid delusions of stealing or hiding things, jealousy or infidelity on the part of the spouse (Jeste and Twamley, 2003). Hallucinations, paranoia and delusions may occur with dementia (Dementia Australia, 2018). There is also misidentification by some people where they don't recognise people or mistake reflections of themselves in the mirror for someone else (Dementia Australia, 2018).

As for all people experiencing changes in behaviour, particularly experiencing things that are imagined by the person and out of touch with reality, the first action to be taken is a medical check to assess the situation and decide what actions should be taken. In the case of older people, it is particularly important that the medical assessment includes the following:

- Eliminating the presence of other physical conditions (such as infections, Parkinson's disease or stroke)
- Eliminating psychiatric conditions such as bipolar disorder
- Checking the effects of medication that the person is currently taking (such as sedatives to reduce agitation and help with sleeping)

Anti-psychotic medication is generally only prescribed if the psychotic symptoms are severe enough to cause distressing agitation or aggression or otherwise disrupt the person's functioning (Cohen-Mansfield, 2001).

Having said this, Chen et al (2010) report in the U.S. setting that 'up to one-third of all nursing home residents, primarily patients with dementia, receive antipsychotic medications for the treatment of symptoms of psychosis, agitation and aggression'. One of the problems with anti-psychotic medications is that they may have side effects such as stiffness, shakiness or drowsiness, so it is best that they are only prescribed if there are major problems, they are introduced slowly at low dosage and the dose is increased slowly to ensure side effects are minimal and the desired results optimal in reducing or eliminating the symptoms of psychosis.

Other and/or additional options for treatment for psychosis in dementia are psychosocial approaches, which include providing support and education to caregivers and environmental modifications to increase the person's orientation and decrease confusion. Such interventions may include optimisation of social contact, increase in structured activities, environmental enrichment, prevention of overstimulation and light therapy (Cohen-Mansfield, 2001).

Supporter vignette — A daughter's experience

Mum was 94. She was in a nursing home. She was easy-going, always happy to see me. She enjoyed participating in the activities in the home. We were both joining in the Melbourne Cup Day celebrations. When I arrived, Mum was sitting up in her chair as usual. I looked at her and could see immediately that she had a face drop. One side of her mouth was droopy, and she was dribbling from that side. I buzzed the nursing staff to tell them Mum had a stroke. She wasn't too bad. We were able to transfer her to a wheelchair, and I took her to the local hospital in my car, knowing that the ambulance would take a long time to come. They admitted her to hospital – did some tests, stabilised her, got her walking again (she was dragging one leg slightly, but that resolved relatively quickly). She had some weakness in her arm. The dribbling worried her most. She was discharged after a few days and returned to the nursing home in my car.

Mum continued to recover over a few weeks, but then her behaviour changed rapidly, with hallucinations and delusions and extreme agitation. She believed she was dead and buried and was extremely distressed, disoriented and anxious. I'd try to distract her by taking her for a walk in the home. She believed that if she walked in one direction, she got older as she walked, and if she walked in the other, she got younger.

As well as being extremely distressing for Mum, it was distressing for us all, including the staff and patients who were all very upset seeing her this way. She was confined to her room, or the director of nursing let her sit with her in her office.

A psycho-geriatrician was called. She conducted an assessment and prescribed anti-psychotics. Mum recovered quickly and lived very happily on her medication for the remaining two years of her life. Her only side effect was weight gain, but she had been underweight, so the weight gain was not a problem. Reducing or ceasing the medication was discussed a couple of times; however, with Mum at 94, there didn't appear to be any point in upsetting the balance and interfering with something that was working well for her.

Early identification and harm minimisation

Getting help early

Whether this is the first time you've experienced concerns about your mental health or you recognise your symptoms from previous episodes, it is important for you to take notice of any changes that you feel in yourself. If you are experiencing any changes in thoughts, feelings or behaviours, you should check it out with someone you trust, particularly if the changes persist or escalate. If either you or your support persons have any concerns, seek medical assistance. You can go to a GP or to the emergency department of your local hospital. If you feel that you need urgent attention because you are getting worse, feeling out of control or feeling suicidal, self-harming or considering harming others, then you should go to the emergency department in your local hospital; ideally, go with someone you trust. Alternatively, phone 000 and ask for an ambulance to take you to hospital.

Remember that the earlier you get help, the quicker you can start treatment and are on the road to recovery. The longer psychosis is left untreated, the more likely you are to have 'slower and less complete recovery, poorer response to antipsychotics, interference with social and psychological development and an increased risk of relapse' (Australian Clinical Guidelines for Early Psychosis, 2010).

Activity: Identifying mental health services near where you live

Start to research sources of assistance for mental health services near where you live. If you don't have a GP, ask your friends who they go to and whether they'd recommend the GP for you. Go to the GP and have a discussion with them. Ask them about health professionals in the area whom you may be able to go to if you need them. Ask them about psychologists and psychiatrists in the area and any other services they can recommend, such as the community mental health team. Talk to the GP about local public and private hospitals and which they'd recommend. Ask the GP about financial support for the treatment of chronic health conditions. Record their recommendations in your contact list on your mobile.

Treatment for early signs of psychosis

The treatment of early signs and symptoms of psychosis generally involves seeing a GP for initial assessment. The GP may refer you to a psychiatrist for further assessment and treatment. The GP may also refer you to other health professionals depending on your concerns. You may, for example, need assistance to work through challenges in your life, or you may have early signs of a mental health condition, such as anxiety or depression, that need treatment, or you may be losing touch with reality, possibly reflecting early signs of the more serious condition of psychosis. It is also worth remembering that even if you have signs of more serious mental health conditions, research indicates that less than one-third of people who meet clinical high-risk criteria actually develop a psychotic illness (Fusar-Poli et al, 2012).

Medications have a role in the lead-up to psychosis, but the first line of pre-psychosis treatment is usually supportive care (McGorry, 2011). Antipsychotics might not be appropriate at this stage, but some medications may help you deal with anxiety, depression and stress to eliminate possible triggers of a psychotic episode.

Be open and honest with your doctor. Tell them about your thoughts, behaviours and moods. Try to tell them each of the symptoms you have and describe the symptoms with examples of what you're thinking, saying, feeling and doing that you feel are different from usual or strange for you. It is unlikely that you will be given a diagnosis in the early stages as symptoms are emerging and changing. The doctor will listen to your symptoms and may refer you to other health professionals who may be able to help you. You may be referred to a psychiatrist for further assessment and treatment. You may be referred to a psychologist if you are feeling overwhelmed about a life event, such as a separation from a life partner or a death in the family. The GP will generally ask you to return if you have any changes to your condition.

Assessment and diagnosis of psychosis

The assessment and diagnosis of mental health conditions are made by psychiatrists. Psychiatrists are medical doctors who have also completed specialist training in mental health. A referral is required to see a psychiatrist. A referral may be obtained from a GP. The GP can also recommend psychiatrists near where you live.

The psychiatrist will do an assessment of you that will include talking with you to take a history and discuss your condition with you, assess your signs, symptoms and risk factors, order tests as appropriate (such as blood tests) and diagnose the mental health condition to determine the most appropriate treatment for the condition. Treatment recommended by the psychiatrist is primarily medication required for your symptoms and diagnosis.

There is no cost to you to see a psychiatrist through the public system; however, appointments may be infrequent and hard to get. A private psychiatrist is expensive, but as soon as you reach the Medicare safety net ($2,093 in 2018), 80 per cent of your costs will be covered by Medicare.

Professional support

You may only need a GP and psychiatrist (and lots of support from family and friends) when you have early signs of psychosis. However, the symptoms and triggers for your symptoms may impact other aspects of your life. It helps to know that there are a range of professionals who can assist you in managing your symptoms, different aspects of your treatment and any challenges or issues in your life. For example, if you have financial difficulties or need help with accommodation, you need to see a social worker. If you need help with your daily activities – such as looking after yourself, cooking, budgeting etc – or are worried about your studies or work, an occupational therapist can help you. A dietician can help you plan out a balanced diet.

The range of health professionals available to you include the following:

- Your general practitioner (GP) — It is good to have a regular GP who knows you and your history, will see you quickly, is well positioned to appreciate any changes or concerns you have and will support you to take action that's recommended
- Psychiatrists — specialist medical doctors who diagnose and treat mental health conditions (primarily with medications)
- Case managers — You may be assigned a case manager after discharge from a public hospital. They are usually psychologists, social workers or occupational therapists or your GP.
- Psychologists — university-qualified professionals who help work through life issues
- Counsellors — also help work through life issues, particularly in specific areas, such as relationships counselling
- Occupational therapists — university-qualified professionals who help with any challenges around activities of daily living, school, work, recreation etc
- Social workers — university-qualified professionals who help sort out issues such as financial support, accommodation etc
- Psychiatric nurses — university-qualified professionals who may be working in mental health hospitals or community mental health teams (they are particularly important contacts in mental health crisis situations)
- Other allied health professionals who may look after other aspects of your mental and psychical health, including chiropractors, optometrists, osteopaths, pharmacists, physiotherapists, podiatrists, audiologists, dietitians, exercise physiologists, music therapists, art therapists, nutritionists, pathologists, sonographers and speech pathologists

Your GP is best positioned to advise you on the most appropriate health professionals to assist and support you with any particular area of concern for you. Your GP is also in the best position to help coordinate your treatment. You may even be able to access financial assistance for the services (go to your GP or a social worker for assistance with this). You can, for example, get a mental healthcare plan from a GP for six to ten sessions with specific treatment goals with a psychologist, occupational therapist, physiotherapist or social worker, and Medicare covers a rebate.

What you can do to help alleviate symptoms

Self-care is important. There are activities you can do to help alleviate symptoms in addition to any treatment prescribed, such as medications. These include the following:

- Questioning your thoughts and experiences
- Recognising early warning signs and taking appropriate action
- Following your treatment plan and taking your medications as prescribed
- Getting a good amount of sleep
- Establishing routines
- Identifying and reducing stress
- Making time for rest and relaxation
- Doing activities that are important to you
- Doing things with others/spending time with your friends and family
- Improving your lifestyle
- Getting the support you need

Question your thoughts and experiences

Questioning your thoughts and experiences is about checking out what you're thinking, feeling or doing with people you trust to make sure they are real and not imagined. Explain what you're feeling to them and check out whether they are fact or fiction. Seek help if the feedback supports that you may be losing touch with reality.

Recognise early warning signs and take appropriate action

Recognise early warning signs of psychosis, such as not sleeping, feeling different, strange, anxious or depressed and hearing or seeing things. Take action as appropriate by discussing them with someone you trust or going to your GP or to the emergency department of the hospital if you need immediate help.

Follow your treatment plan and take medication as prescribed

It is important to follow your treatment plan and take medication as prescribed. Medication may have unpleasant side effects, but the side effects are better than having an episode of psychosis. Stopping or missing medication may impact your recovery and/or cause problems from sudden withdrawal of the medication.

Self-soothe to distract yourself from symptoms

Bearing in mind that you should also seek professional help for your symptoms, you can potentially reduce symptoms or distract from your symptoms by 'self-soothing'.

Self-soothing involves using your five senses (sight, touch, smell, taste and hearing) to distract yourself from your symptoms and help reduce distress. Examples of activities you can try include the following:

- Sight: watching a sunrise or focusing on treasured photos
- Touch: playing with a stress ball, a bangle or a treasured item in your pocket or stroking your cat or dog
- Smell: lighting a scented candle
- Taste: cooking your favourite meal, drinking herbal tea
- Hearing: playing a chill-out compilation

You can also work out ways of distracting yourself from some of the more severe signs, such as hallucinations. Examples of activities that may help distract you include the following:

- Doing additions, subtractions, divisions and multiplications in your head
- Counting backwards in your head from a high number or counting in units of three, four, five etc or counting backwards in units of three, four, five etc
- Grounding exercises like saying your name, where you are and what you did today
- Closing your eyes and paying attention to your breathing (in and out breaths)
- Giving voices in your head a silly name to diffuse them
- Reading something backwards
- Doing intense exercise, but if running, use a treadmill or running track so you don't have an accident
- Humming a song multiple times
- Keeping a diary of when the voices come and avoiding situations when this usually happens
- Picking up your phone and pretending to talk to the voices to instruct them to go away

Get a good amount of sleep

It is recommended that adults have seven to nine hours of sleep per night. Getting a good amount of sleep is critical to maintaining your well-being. A change in your sleep patterns leading to difficulty sleeping may be a critical early warning sign of deterioration in your mental well-being. Lack of sleep may be a significant factor in tipping you over into psychosis. Seek help early if this symptom persists. The following suggestions may help you get into a regular pattern of good sleep.

- Set a regular time to go to bed and wake up
- Get some morning sunshine, which helps your body clock
- Exercise during the day so you are tired at night
- Don't take naps during the day if they interfere with sleep at night
- Avoid caffeine after 3:00 p.m.
- Avoid alcohol before bed as it disturbs sleeping patterns
- Limit screen time just before bed as it can be overstimulating, and the blue light, in most devices, makes your brain think it is daytime

- Don't watch TV or read in bed; make your bed a place designated just for sleep
- Take a warm bath or shower before bed to unwind
- Try meditation or mindfulness to relax before bed
- Use earplugs and an eye mask if needed
- Try to avoid sleeping pills unless you miss a lot of sleep
- If you can't sleep after thirty minutes of trying, read a book and then go back to bed
- See a doctor or sleep clinic if nothing seems to work

Establish routines

When your world is changing around you and you may be feeling insecure and fearful, it is important to try to regain a semblance of 'normal'. You may be taking time out from your studies or work; however, it is still important to establish routines and do things that give you pleasure.

Establishing or re-establishing routines can help you feel more secure and safe and give you a feeling of normalising your life. To establish routines, you can start by establishing a regular pattern around sleeping and waking. Your symptoms and medication may make it difficult for you to get up in the morning. Set a reasonable time that you'll get up at each day. This does not need to be early in the morning, just a regular pattern. Wake up to things you enjoy. Wake up to your favourite music playing. Walk to your favourite café for coffee each morning. Catch up on social media or meet friends in the café. Plan your day. Set small goals. Do things you enjoy doing. Congratulate yourself on what you've achieved during your day.

Identify and reduce stress

Having symptoms of psychosis and feeling different and strange is stressful. The impacts of your symptoms, such as believing that people are talking about you, may also contribute to your stress. You are also likely to be out of your regular routines, which may contribute to your anxiety and insecurity. Acknowledge that you aren't well, give yourself permission to take things easy and be gentle with yourself. Try to re-establish routines and maintain your usual standards of personal health and hygiene.

There may be stressors in your life that are contributing to your anxiety or depression or causing early signs of psychosis. Stressors may be associated with areas such as your studies, work or relationships or being unwell and unable to do your usual activities. The first step is to identify the stressors in your life. You may need help to do this. Your GP or a psychologist can help you identify the stressors in your life and work out a plan and program to eliminate the sources of stress or reduce your stress and help alleviate your symptoms. Depending on the sources of your stress, your stress reduction plan may include the following:

- Using relaxation techniques to lower your stress
- Enrolling in a course on lowering stress in your life or other related areas such as mindfulness
- Joining a group such as yoga or Pilates classes
- Taking a sick leave to give yourself time to recover
- Working with a counsellor, psychologist or social worker to help address challenges in your life
- Meeting with your supervisor at work to adjust your role (such as changing your role to work on a specific project for a period), change your job description (such as giving some of your tasks to others), assign varying working hours for a period (such as working part-time or job sharing) or make you work from home for a period
- Talking to your teachers to explain your situation and request considerations, such as adjusting assessment types or extending assignment deadlines
- Reducing the number of study units or going from full-time study to part-time or extending your completion dates

Activity: De-stressing your life

Identify stressors in your life and create a plan for eliminating or alleviating them.

Make time for rest and relaxation

Stress and anxiety can make any problem seem worse. Try to reduce stress and anxiety by giving yourself time to rest and relax.

Do activities that are important to you

If you are feeling 'strange' and confused and a little fearful of what is happening to you, it is important for you to understand the activities that distract you from your fears, that make you feel like your 'normal' self, that reassure and comfort you and that you enjoy doing. There are a broad range of activities that may be as simple as the following:

- Thinking about what you enjoy doing or reliving an event you enjoyed in your head
- Playing a game on your laptop, such as chess, scrabble or computer games
- Writing a blog post or posting on social media
- Phoning or texting family and friends
- Visiting family or friends
- Joining a group
- Watching a video
- Listening to music
- Singing and/or dancing
- Exercising (such as on treadmill or bike), Pilates or yoga
- Swimming, going for a walk or playing a team sport
- Playing an instrument
- Doing a puzzle (e.g. jigsaw)
- Cooking
- Gardening
- Reading or reciting poetry
- Joining an amateur actors group
- Art making, such as painting, colouring in, drawing or making digital art
- Knitting or sewing

- Activities like playing with a child or your pet or going to a movie with a friend

Activity: Identify activities that give you pleasure

At the end of each day, consider what you've enjoyed doing in your day. Compile a list of these activities and go through them when you feel the need. Do activities that make you feel better.

Do things with others/spend time with your friends and family

Experiencing the symptoms of psychosis may be isolating. Make an effort to remain in contact with your family and friends, even if it is primarily through social media or text messages. Your family and friends care for you. They may worry when they don't hear from you. It is important for you and your family and friends that you contact them regularly to let them know how you are and what you're doing.

It is also likely that your family and friends are feeling confused and distressed about the changes they are seeing in you. Doing 'normal', enjoyable activities may be reassuring for you and your family and friends. All of you may feel a little better and more connected, and it may give you and them an opportunity to talk and/or simply enjoy being together.

Improve your lifestyle

Try simple changes to your life to make healthier choices about food, alcohol and exercise. Try reducing your alcohol intake, eating three good meals a day, not eating between meals, eating smaller portions of food or going for a walk every day at the same time. Celebrate your successes.

Lived experience vignette — Mark's early warning signs of psychosis

For me, I was initially depressed. Then a busy period of work came up, and I couldn't sleep. I felt detached from reality and lost confidence in my work. I asked others for help but couldn't explain what I was feeling in an organised and clear way. I have schizoaffective disorder, meaning that sometimes I have had psychosis by itself, sometimes with an elevated mood (hypomania or mania) and sometimes with depression. So predicting psychosis is difficult because it could happen when I am extremely happy, extremely sad or completely devoid of emotions. Even so, there were clear warning signs that I needed help. I was suicidal and had a plan to kill myself. I saw a doctor, and he prescribed antidepressants, but he only spent eight minutes with me, so I didn't trust his prescription. After a period of depression, I had several sleepless nights and couldn't do my job properly. I became manic first and then delusional with paranoia.

When I had first become depressed, I did the right thing and went to a GP. When I became anxious at work, I informed my manager and got help from a free psychologist through the employee assistance program (EAP). Then when I became manic, I went back to the GP and got a referral to a psychiatrist. Many men do not seek help so quickly, if at all, but even with these interventions, I got sicker and eventually became psychotic. Had my carers or I recognised my delusions early, I would have got on antipsychotics sooner and avoided the more severe paranoid and persecutory delusions.

Finding support persons

It is particularly important to have trusted support persons in the case of psychosis as the symptoms of psychosis may mean that you are out of touch with reality in some areas of your life and you need people you can check this out with. Additionally, in the case of psychosis, symptoms may escalate quickly, and you may need trusted persons who understand this and act quickly to get the right assistance for you. Unfortunately, it may also be the case that symptoms of psychosis recur, and you need trusted persons who appreciate this and can give you feedback and help you take appropriate action. Unfortunately, it may also be the case that you don't always treat your support persons respectfully because you believe your delusions are real and you have no insight into your condition as it becomes more severe. This places a lot of pressure on support persons, who may need to act against your will at times for your own good.

The most obvious support persons are family members. The other option is friends. You may also join support groups to share your experience with others in similar situations. You need to identify family members and friends whom you feel closest to. You need to meet with them and ask them whether they'll help support you through your symptoms. You need to have an honest and open conversation with them about what this means. The role of support persons includes the following:

- Being available to talk with you about your symptoms and the help you need
- Giving you feedback about whether your thoughts, feelings and beliefs are real or imagined
- Discussing what actions (if any) need to be taken and assisting you to take those actions
- Being available to support you with your treatment plan
- Being available to support you in making other changes you're trying to make in your life, such as eating sensibly, reducing alcohol intake, doing more exercise etc
- Keeping an eye on you and alerting you about any observations they've made about you
- Being positive and celebrating successes
- Doing fun things together

Being a support person can be demanding and thankless at times. As a person who experiences psychotic episodes, you have some responsibilities to your supporters. You need to respect that they do care and worry about you. You need to establish a communication regime with them to let them know what's happening with you. You need to talk about this with them. When you are not feeling well, you may need to agree to text them once each day to let them know what's happening.

You also need to try to retain a respectful relationship with your supporters even when you are unwell. Your illness is not an excuse for disrespectful behaviour. You may be angry, confused and distressed and feel like taking it out on someone. Your supporters are obvious targets. When you are feeling like taking out your anger on your supporters, try to stop yourself and work out strategies for not behaving badly towards them. These may be strategies such as walking away from the person and using distracting techniques that work for you, such as playing with an object (e.g. a ring or a bangle), carrying a worry stone in your pocket, diverting yourself by playing solitaire online or thinking about your favourite scene, person or event and replaying it in your head. Other distractions may be counting backwards in your head or using relaxation techniques.

Support persons may themselves need support to fulfil this role. They may like to join groups of support persons or join online forums of support persons through organisations such as SANE or the Mental Health Carers Association in your state.

The role of support persons in the early stages of psychosis

If you think someone is acting strangely or differently, you need to act on this, particularly if it persists or gets worse. Your primary goal is to get them to a medical practitioner who can assess them and take appropriate medical action. The sooner you can do this, the better the outcome is likely to be. The person may not want to seek help and may resist help. It may be difficult for you because you care for the person and want to retain their trust, but you also need to get them to a medical practitioner for a professional assessment.

Try to be calm and supportive. Listen to what they have to say. They may be feeling confused and frightened. Empathise with them about their feeling. Don't be judgemental. Help them stay safe and feel secure. You may be able to give them practical help with activities they are finding difficult, such as getting to school or work or paying bills. This all helps maintain their trust; however, remember that your main goal is to get them to a medical practitioner. This is frequently very stressful for you and the person you care for.

If you notice early warning signs, try to check if other signs are also present. You want to be able to inform medical practitioners of these symptoms if you are given permission to talk to them. Some people with psychosis may downplay their symptoms or feel intimidated by medical professionals, so if you can't speak with professionals directly, try to remind the person you are supporting of symptoms they can mention.

Sometimes it's difficult to have conversations with friends or workmates about their mental health, particularly if you're worried about them. You can use the free Beyond Blue Check-in app (www.youthbeyondblue.com/ help-someone-you-know/thecheckin) to help plan out the conversation you feel you need to have with the person.

Activity: Supporter's observations

Keep a record of the symptoms you see in the person you are supporting. Keep the specific examples of the symptoms. Discuss these with the person. If the person denies them, ask them to go with you to their GP and discuss them together.

Supporter vignette — A partner's experience of a first episode of psychosis

Shortly after Mark's 30th birthday, he changed jobs. He mentioned he was annoyed with some of the people he worked with, but I didn't notice any major problems. He worked some late nights teaching, and Sydney Uni failed to give him Fridays as a research day, which his supervisor had promised him. He saw an EAP counsellor and then decided to resign, but his contract had a ridiculous twenty-six-week notice period. We were also selling our apartment, which was stressful for both of us because it had rented furniture in it, so we had to live with Mark's mum. He was really stressed one day and so took a sick leave.

It was the Queen's birthday, a long weekend in 2016, when things got really out of hand. On the Thursday before the long weekend, he called me saying he was paranoid. Then when we met up, he was obsessed with cameras watching him. He spoke about footage being subpoenaed to use in a case against the university. He then explained about his very stressful day at work, his seeking of help from a friend who had failed to calm him and his suicidal ideation.

Supporter vignette — A mum's experience of a first episode of psychosis

Mark has always been entrepreneurial, driven, full of ideas and busy with lots of ventures, carrying them through to fruition, climbing mountains and delivering. I love this in him. He is always positive and encouraging, always ready to help, there for me when I need a hand with IT or want some support for my own ideas.

He was 30 when he had had his first psychotic episode. He was having trouble sleeping. He was working on his laptop in the middle of the night. I sat with him. He was distressed and crying about his friend who was on drugs. He wanted to save his friend. He wanted to act immediately. He was agitated. I could only sit with him and help him get through the night.

He was working as a uni lecturer with a team of four. Two of the team were off on stress leave. It was exam time. The students all wanted help. Mark's phone was ringing constantly; students were lined up to see him. He felt overwhelmed and ran out into the fire stairs, unable to cope any longer. Everything started to unravel relatively quickly after that. Mark tipped over from 'busy' to more of a frenzy of activity. Mark was falling apart in front of our eyes. Mark's partner Ray and I were bewildered, struggling to cope with Mark's symptoms. We sought help from GPs, but I don't think they understood how seriously ill he was. We didn't really know how to get help for him.

Achieving wellness

The symptoms of psychosis vary greatly and may impact many aspects of your life, including physical, psychological and social aspects of your life. They can also impact on what you do, whether that be activities of your daily life – such as being able to go out, go to school, go to uni or go to work – or going out with other people or participating in recreational, sporting or entertainment activities. When you are having early symptoms of psychosis, it may be helpful to consider the impacts the symptoms are having on your life and seek help to address them early. The following table may help you to work out your priorities and actions that you can take to help alleviate some of the symptoms you may be experiencing as well as making healthy choices and improving your lifestyle.

Mental health is not merely the absence of disease. Achieving 'mental health' involves actively working on all aspects of your life throughout your life to achieve a healthy and fulfilling life.

Plan for living life well

Aspects of life	Goal	Treatment	Support persons
Whole of life	To achieve a state of well-being by eliminating symptoms, preventing recurrences and living life well, dealing with challenges as they arise to lead a productive and enjoyable life, which includes making a contribution to your community		
Physical health and well-being	To be physically well and free from physical disease and in a position to function well to reach your potential in your community	• Screening for symptoms of chronic diseases, such as diabetes, raised cholesterol, heart disease, obesity • Immunisations such as flu vaccine, shingles, pneumococcal vaccine, meningococcal vaccine, human papilloma virus (HPV) vaccine etc • Dental care • Healthy lifestyle, including healthy eating, physical activity, proper sleep and reducing unhealthy habits such as smoking, alcohol and drugs	Family/friends Psychiatrist General practitioner Medical specialists Dentist Psychologist Physiotherapist Dietician Personal trainer/gym
Psychological health and well-being	To be cognitively healthy (the way we think), emotionally healthy (the way we feel) and socially healthy (have healthy relationships) so that you can reach your potential, cope with the normal stresses of life, work productively and fruitfully and make a contribution to your community	• Assessment by a GP to determine what help you may need and/or referral for additional services, such as referral to a psychiatrist • Assessment and diagnosis of condition by a psychiatrist and development of a treatment plan (as appropriate) • Establishing a relationship with a case manager, such as a community health worker or GP who can coordinate your treatment plan • Working with a psychologist to develop a plan to manage your symptoms, which includes staying well	Family/friends Psychologist Life coach/mentor Community health worker Social worker Occupational therapist Counsellor Cognitive behaviour therapist Psychiatrist General practitioner

		• Working with your health professional team and support persons to implement your treatment plan, including the following:
		   • Medication to reduce your symptoms and recover (psychiatrist)
		   • Psychological support as needed (psychologist)
		   • Therapy (as appropriate)
		• Establishing a relationship with a health professional, such as a psychologist, to identify your life goals, establish priorities and endeavour to address achievable goals in your life	

Social health and well-being	To have good personal and social relationships so that you are not isolated, feel good about yourself, feel connected with others and feel part of your community	• Working with a psychologist to develop and implement a plan for maintaining and building your social network and establishing a range of activities that you enjoy doing • Maintaining and building a network of family and friends whom you trust who can provide you with support and feedback and do activities with you • Counselling and support for reinforcing healthy relationships and managing challenges with interpersonal relationships • Joining and participating in support groups as appropriate • Participating in online forums as appropriate • Joining recreational, sporting or hobby groups	Family/friends Psychologist Counsellor Social worker Occupational therapist Life coach/mentor General practitioner Psychiatrist Community health worker

	Goals	Strategies	Resources
Daily living	To be able to manage daily living tasks, such as money, self-care, housekeeping, cooking, laundry, transport and shopping To have adequate accommodation and finances to be able to finance treatment and lead a reasonable life	• Working with a social worker in regard to assistance with accommodation, financial support etc as needed • Working with Centrelink to organise social security and other services, such as income support, sickness allowance, mobility allowance, payment support for job seekers etc • Working with an occupational therapist to develop and implement a plan for addressing challenging areas of daily living, such as shopping or managing transport • Joining support groups focusing on cooking, budgeting etc • Participating in training in areas such as cooking and budgeting	Family/friends Occupational therapist Social worker Centrelink Community education TAFE colleges
Recreation, education and work	To be able to achieve your full potential and make a contribution to your community	• Working with your health professional team, such as occupational therapist and psychologist, to identify issues and challenges with your studies/work/ activities and developing and implementing a plan to address these • Working with your school, university or manager and HR at work to discuss your condition and identify any accommodations that need to be made, such as special assistance with assessment, extending assessment dates, working at home, revising your job description, changing your hours of work etc • Talking to your teachers to explain your situation and request considerations such as adjusting assessment types or extending assignment deadlines	Family/friends Occupational therapist Psychologist Vocational counsellor School/university counsellor Centrelink

- Reducing the number of study units or going from full-time study to part-time or extending your completion dates
- Taking a sick leave to recover from stressful periods
- Meeting with your supervisor at work to adjust your role (such as changing your role to work on a specific project for a period), change your job description (such as giving some of your tasks to others), assign varying working hours for a period (such as working part-time or job sharing) or make you work from home for a period
- Establishing a relationship with a health professional, such as a psychologist, to identify your life goals, establish priorities and endeavour to address achievable goals in your life
- Working with your health professional team to develop and implement a plan for establishing a range of activities that you enjoy doing
- Joining a sport, recreational or hobby group
- Joining a gym or working with a personal trainer
- Consulting a dietician or joining Weight Watchers or a similar group
- Doing activities with your family and friends that you enjoy doing
- Doing community education classes or a course at TAFE

Choosing a healthy lifestyle

Medical assessment and treatment such as medication and therapy is always the priority for symptoms of psychosis. Self-care is also important. You can start thinking about your own lifestyle and whether there are factors in your lifestyle – such as excessive alcohol, smoking, poor eating habits, sedentary lifestyle or abuse of drugs – that may be contributing to your condition. By committing to healthier lifestyle choices, you may be able to help alleviate your symptoms and reduce the risk of future episodes. You can also reduce the risk of developing lifestyle diseases such as heart disease and diabetes, lung cancer as a consequence of smoking, liver disease as a consequence of alcohol abuse, psychotic episodes as a potential consequence of drug abuse and much more. It is hard to change long-standing habits, but the consequences of not changing have escalated with the diagnosis of a mental health condition.

You can seek professional help to make healthy lifestyle changes. Depending on the changes you want to make, you can receive professional help from your GP, psychologist, gym, personal trainer or dietician. You can google Australian government bodies that give advice on making lifestyle changes (such as state and federal departments of health). You can google the professional associations of relevant areas (such as the Dieticians Association of Australia at daa.asn.au). You can join groups such as Alcoholics Anonymous, Weight Watchers and fitness groups or take up a sport; swimming is particularly good because it is low impact and exercises a lot of muscle groups. You can join online support groups.

You may also be eligible for financial support to make these changes through the Chronic Diseases Management Plan (available through a search at health.gov.au). Your GP can help you make sensible choices.

Avoiding alcohol and illicit drugs

Avoiding alcohol and illicit drugs helps you stay well. Drugs and alcohol may have direct and indirect impacts on your health and well-being. They may, for example, interact with your other medications, making them work less effectively or causing unpredictable outcomes. Complete abstinence is usually a lot more effective than saying you are just going to have one or two drinks or 'just one joint' as it's easy to binge after that first step of becoming uninhibited. It is difficult to break long-standing habits. You need professional help and support to achieve this. You can also join support groups such as Alcoholics Anonymous, Family Drug Support and SMART Recovery Australia.

One method from dialectical behaviour therapy (DBT) and other mindfulness-based programs to reduce cravings is 'urge surfing', which involves the following:

1. Thinking of urges like waves in the ocean (They come and go, and you don't have to act on the urge. As you learn to 'urge-surf', the waves won't crash down on you. Urges are small when they start, they peak, and then they subside.)
2. Watching your breath without changing your pattern of breathing
3. Noticing your thoughts and any cravings you have
4. Identifying the part of your body where you most feel the craving
5. Removing yourself from situations that lead to the craving if you can
6. Using a mantra to emphasise that cravings are temporary, like 'This will pass'
7. Observing how your craving eventually subsides, which is natural and inevitable because of how your brain works (With practice, cravings will be less intense and easier to surf.)

You might also decide to quit smoking as part of your recovery. People who have experienced psychosis are much more likely to smoke, with 66.6 per cent (72 per cent of men and 59 per cent of women) of all people with psychosis smoking (Cooper et al, 2012). As well as the extremely harmful physical health consequences of smoking, there is evidence that smoking actually causes stress, even though it seems like it relieves it. The quitnow government resource can help you find effective ways to quit. Your community mental health team may also be able to help provide Nicorette or Nicabate for free or for a subsidised cost.

Healthy eating

Both the symptoms of complex mental health conditions and some of the medications may increase weight gain, compounding the impact of symptoms of psychosis on confidence and self-esteem. It is therefore important to establish healthy eating patterns as early as possible to try to mitigate the possible effects of psychotic episodes. Healthy eating can help improve the quality of life and well-being and provides protection against some chronic diseases, such as heart disease, stroke and diabetes.

The Australian Dietary Guidelines make the following recommendations in regard to healthy eating. To achieve and maintain a healthy weight, be physically active and choose amounts of nutritious food and drinks to meet your energy needs. Enjoy a wide variety of nutritious foods from these five groups every day:

1. Plenty of vegetables
2. Fruit
3. Grain (cereal) foods, mostly wholegrain and/or high cereal fibre varieties, such as breads, rice, pasta, noodles, oats and quinoa
4. Lean meats and poultry, fish, eggs, tofu, nuts, seeds and legumes/beans
5. Milk, yoghurt and cheese, mostly reduced fat (and plenty of water)

Limit intake of foods containing saturated fat, added salt, added sugars and alcohol.

Limit intake of foods high in saturated fat, such as biscuits, cakes, pastries, pies, processed meats, commercial burgers, pizza, fried foods, potato chips, crisps and other savoury snacks. Replace high-fat foods that contain predominantly saturated fats, such as butter, cream, cooking margarine, and coconut and palm oil as well as foods that contain predominantly polyunsaturated and monounsaturated fats, including oils, spreads, peanut butter and avocado.

Seek help from a professional such as a dietician to develop a plan for healthy eating and provide support for you to implement it. You can find a dietician near you by going to the Dieticians Association of Australia (see daa.asn.au). You may also find support through a group such as Weight Watchers Australia or online support groups for weight loss. Many groups can be found on Meetup.com and Facebook.

Your GP can also help you find a dietician in your area who may be able to work with you. Your GP may also be able to organise financial support through the Chronic Diseases Management Plan (see health.gov.au).

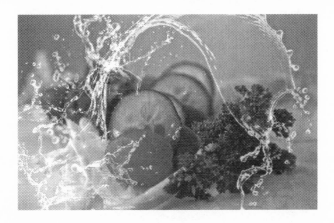

Exercise

The old adage is 'healthy body, healthy mind'. The physical benefits of exercise are well documented. They include reducing the risk of heart disease, stroke, type 2 diabetes, some cancers, arthritis and excessive weight gain. The benefits of exercise in the treatment of depression are also well documented. A 2017 international study by the Black Dog Institute recommended that as little as one hour a week of exercise may protect against depression.

Research supports the benefits of exercise for other mental health conditions considering that those with complex mental health conditions such as schizophrenia have an average life expectancy twelve to fifteen years less than the general population. Factors contributing to this disparity include the higher rate of suicide as well as risk factors associated with an unhealthy lifestyle. Other factors include symptoms of the illness, such as depression, and side effects of medication, such as lack of motivation, weight gain and increased risk of damage to some organs. Some research indicates that exercise changes levels of endorphins, which lift the mood, and serotonin, which helps regulate the mood, appetite, digestion, memory and sleep. For example, a study from the University of Queensland indicated that regular exercise boosted mood and tendency to look on the bright side.

The Department of Health recommends about half to one hour per day of moderate activity. Moderate activity includes brisk walking, swimming, social tennis and dancing. Alternatively, you can do one and one quarter or two and a half hours per week of vigorous activity, such as aerobics, jogging or competitive sports (that make you puff and unable to talk at the same time as doing the exercises).

If you aren't used to exercising, you should start exercising gently (for example, by walking), without overexertion, and gradually build up towards reaching recommended levels. Aim to be active on every day of the week if possible.

Activity: Changing your lifestyle

List the aspects of your life that you'd like to change. Prioritise the aspects that are most important for you to change. Decide where you'd like to start. Focus on your top priorities. Identify how you are going to get the help you need to make changes to these aspects of your life. Take the first step and make the initial contacts to start you on your journey. Start by setting yourself small achievable goals and reward yourself when you achieve them. Don't beat yourself up if you break out every now and then. Just get back on board and continue. Get the support you need to help you.

Managing a psychotic episode

Symptoms in acute psychosis

According to the DSM-5 and other reputable sources, delusions and hallucinations are very common in the acute phase of psychosis.

Delusions

Delusions are beliefs in something untrue that do not change even with evidence to the contrary. Delusions may involve the following:

- Persecutory delusions, such as thinking there is someone out to harm you
- Delusions of reference, such as if a billboard seems like it has a special message for you
- Delusions of surveillance, where you feel like you are being watched and recorded
- Delusions of grandeur, such as thinking you have superhuman abilities
- Religious delusions, where you believe the spiritual world is influencing you in some way separate from normal religious beliefs
- Delusional memories, where you think something happened to you in the past that didn't
- Erotomanic delusions, where you falsely believe someone is in love with you
- Somatic delusions, where you falsely believe you have a disease
- Delusional misidentification, where you believe someone is an imposter or someone you know has been replaced by a lookalike
- Delusions of thought interference, where you believe someone is controlling or listening to your thoughts

Hallucinations

Hallucinations also come in many different forms:

- Visual hallucinations, which are vivid and clear depictions of something that doesn't exist
- Auditory hallucinations, which include hearing voices or sounds that aren't there
- Olfactory hallucinations, where you smell odours (usually unpleasant odours) that don't exist
- Tactile hallucinations, where you feel like you are being touched when you are not, as in the common drug-induced psychosis of feeling bugs crawling on you
- Somatic hallucinations of feelings in your body that aren't real
- Gustatory hallucinations, where you taste something that isn't there

Hearing voices is a very common hallucination and, with conditions such as schizophrenia, may persist despite medications. Some people mishear people in crowds. These can be difficult to question because the conversations may be audible to you and others, but what is actually said may be questionable. Others hear voices inside their head which they may attribute to a higher power, aliens or an inner guide.

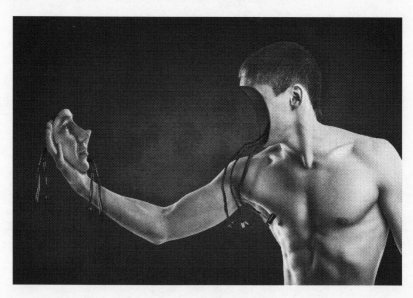

Lived experience vignette — Mark's experience of an acute psychotic episode

When I was first psychotic, I initially had persecutory delusions that I was being framed for a crime. I then had delusions of grandeur that I had worked out a way to cure PTSD. In hospital, I had further persecutory delusions that terrorists had planted a bomb inside me and hijacked the hospital. After the intense fear of terrorism subsided, I went back to grandiosity and thought Ellen was talking to me through the TV. I also think I had olfactory hallucinations because I smelt the worst farts ever from other patients, but perhaps they actually did have disgusting farts from the awful hospital food!

Lived experience vignette — Jamie's experience of an acute psychotic episode

I didn't realise it at the time, but I started looking for more meaning in my life and asking more questions and probably answering my own questions with ideas of things that I didn't really know much about, and I felt this overwhelming belief in ideas that just weren't rational and that kind of led to the condition of psychosis, believing in irrational ideas of being someone that I wasn't, and in that sense, I ended up in hospital. The experience was quite traumatic, and then that experience of being in hospital, given medication, it really knocked me for six. I was out of the park, I couldn't talk properly, I couldn't function properly, and then in relation to my experience around mental health challenges, it was a family – it was a genetic component to it, with other family members being unwell as well, and knowing what they had gone through, I just felt like I had lost my life from everything that I knew, so every time from then and for a number of years, I was in and out of hospital, and my cycle was every time I tried to work again, I would get unwell. I would start working, maybe last two weeks, maybe three or four, and then I would be unwell again. And then I would go into a hospital with psychosis, and then after coming out of hospital, I'd be in a depression. I'd isolate myself, just stay at home. The only people I saw were doctors for doctor's appointments and case managers, and for about five years, four or five years, I was in that cycle.

And surprisingly enough, I had a case manager who just started with me, and she believed in me. And she was encouraging me to get out into the community, I didn't know about community organisations that supported people with mental health challenges, and I felt I owed her because she believed in me so much. I felt that I owed her to give it a chance, and through that, the opportunity came where I was able to connect with others who understood what it was like.

Diagnosis of the condition

Diseases of the psyche have always been slippery things. Schizophrenia, bipolar disorder, major depression and a host of others have no visible markers in the brain. Their symptoms overlap sufficiently that diagnosis may differ between medical practitioners or even vary over time when given by a single practitioner.

— *The Economist* (30/6/18)

As mentioned earlier, diagnosis of the mental health condition is made by a psychiatrist. A psychiatrist is a doctor who specialises in mental health. In the community setting, a person needs a referral from a GP to see a psychiatrist. In the hospital setting, the person will be allocated a hospital psychiatrist. Psychiatrists meet with the person, conduct an assessment, diagnose the condition, generally prescribe medication and develop a treatment plan. Diagnosis of the condition is important because it enables the psychiatrist to determine your treatment plan. It is the first step in your pathway to recovery.

The psychiatrist makes the diagnosis and treatment plan by engaging with the person and their support persons over a period. The diagnosis is made on the basis of the person's

- Personal and medical history (symptoms and context of symptoms, physical and mental health history, family history, substance use, allergies, adverse drug reactions etc)
- Mental state (including appearance, behaviour, speech, mood, affect, cognitive impairment, thought abnormalities, concentration)
- Risk (including risk of harm to self or others, risk of discontinuing treatment)
- Other conditions that may also be present (such as depression, anxiety, cardiovascular disease, diabetes etc)
- Other conditions that may complicate or worsen outcomes (such as substance abuse, cardiovascular disease, liver disease, thyroid disease) [Investigations may include brain imaging (such as MRI), ECG, blood tests (including liver function, thyroid function, anaemia, renal function, glucose levels for diabetes etc) and a urine test for illegal (ice/methamphetamine, cannabis, amphetamines, cocaine) and legal (alcohol, benzodiazepine) drugs. This test should be done for all patients to eliminate substance abuse.]

Diagnosis and treatment is an ongoing process of getting to know the person and their signs and symptoms and the impact of the condition on the person's life. The diagnosis may change over time.

A consumer's vignette — Mark's changing diagnosis

It's hard enough for the professionals to diagnose! My diagnosis started as mania on initial presentation in the public hospital and then later that month as social phobias, generalised anxiety disorder and acute and transient psychotic disorder, unspecified. A month later, with the same public hospital doctor, it was just a single diagnosis of 'mental health disorder'. Two months after that, a new private psychiatrist said it was schizophrenia. Another month later, it was schizoaffective disorder. Yet another private psychiatrist said bipolar. A new public psychiatrist said he couldn't determine whether it was schizoaffective or bipolar. A psychiatry professor who treated me said he didn't believe schizoaffective disorder actually exists! My excellent GP didn't include a diagnosis in my notes because he knew it would change and didn't want me to have a stigmatised label on my medical certificates.

It's important not to self-diagnose, but after seeing so many professionals in the course of my treatment and looking through notes from each of them, I have compared my symptoms and symptom durations with the main manual of diagnosis (the DSM-5) to conclude that I do have schizoaffective disorder. There is a problem with that conclusion as the DSM-5 also says schizoaffective might not actually be its own category of disorder!

Adjusting to your diagnosis

After suffering the symptoms of psychosis and not understanding what is going on, receiving a diagnosis is generally a relief. You realise that your symptoms are part of an illness. Your symptoms are not your fault. You are not a bad person. You are not alone. You can read up on your condition. You can connect with others via social media or in support groups. You can do things to help yourself. You can make choices about your treatment.

You may also have some negative feelings about your diagnosis. You may have a 'serious' mental illness. You have a 'label' that you may know almost nothing about except that the label has many negative connotations and that people may change the way they look at you.

Think of your diagnosis as an illness that you are currently experiencing. It is a name for a set of symptoms. It does not define you as a person. Having a diagnosis of asthma or breaking your arm doesn't define you as a person. Think of your mental illness in the same way as a diagnosis of asthma or a broken arm. Your diagnosis can help you learn about your condition and do something about it.

Some things you can do to help you adjust to your diagnosis include the following:

- Meet with your psychiatrist to discuss your illness, treatment and pathway to recovery

- Connect with others with the illness via social media
- Join a support group
- Educate yourself about your illness
- Share your story with people you trust
- Discuss your feelings with health professionals such as a psychologist, social worker or occupational therapist

Getting the person to treatment in acute episodes of psychosis

People with symptoms of psychosis may present to a GP or the emergency department of a public hospital, seeking help with their symptoms. They may present because they are worried about the changes in themselves or because their symptoms are very distressing. They may present because they are fearful of self-harming or because they are harming themselves, for example self-medicating or abusing drugs or alcohol.

Presentation is often initiated by others because they are worried about the person's condition. The person may not have insight into their condition and may not believe that they need help. It is best if they do go together to a GP or the emergency department of a hospital where a medical practitioner can make an informed assessment of the condition. In this case, it is critical that the person accompanying them participates in the assessment process.

If the person is at risk of harming themselves or others, they need urgent help. Hopefully, the support person can explain this to the person, and they will agree to go to hospital together. If the person does not consent to go to hospital, then the support person may need to phone 000 and seek help from the police and ambulance. The police can assist if they feel the person is at risk of harming themselves or others. They will come and escort the ill person to hospital.

It is always difficult if the person exhibiting symptoms doesn't consent to seek treatment because of their lack of insight into their condition. In this case, the support person needs to assess the level of risk and take appropriate action. This is generally an extremely stressful situation for both the support person and the person they care for. The support person doesn't want to betray the trust of the person they care for, but they recognise that their loved one is severely unwell and may be a danger to themselves and/or to others. They may, in fact, be a danger to their support persons, whom they love dearly when they are well.

For support persons placed in this position, it is helpful to make joint decisions in association with other support persons (such as the whole family). Another option is to phone the community mental health crisis team in your area and explain the situation and request their professional assessment of the situation. The community mental health crisis team can conduct a home visit and assess whether the person needs hospitalisation. In this event, with the cooperation of the person, they can escort them to the emergency department in the hospital. If the team assesses that the person is a danger to themselves or others, they will contact the police and ask for a police escort to accompany the person to the emergency department of the nearest public hospital. This may mean that the person needs to be held involuntarily in the hospital for a period.

It is important that a person who is very unwell is not left alone while support people are trying to get assistance for the person, especially if the ill person is likely to harm themselves. It may, in fact, be better for more than one person to be with them if they are threatening other people. However, the level of danger to others needs to be assessed. One or more of the support persons may, in fact, trigger the escalation of symptoms. If the danger to people with them is too great, then it's best that they are left alone in a place where the ill person feels safe, and the support persons can watch from a distance until assistance arrives.

The most difficult situation is when the person acts on their delusions in a public forum. They may, for example, be in a manic state and be doing strange things that scare people around them, or they may be confronting people who are the subject of their delusions. These situations are rare but are dangerous, particularly for the person with the condition, because they are out of touch with reality and not in a position to be able to evaluate what is going on around them. The person acting on the delusion may also be highly at risk if the police are called.

This is a very good reason why symptoms of psychosis need to be managed as early as possible, before they have escalated to full-blown psychotic episodes that are potentially a danger to themselves and others and may potentially have catastrophic outcomes.

Hospitalisation

Public hospitals

Hospitalisation is very common for acute psychosis. The best option is that the person with the symptoms of psychosis recognises their need for hospitalisation and goes voluntarily to hospital. They will generally be assessed in the emergency department and, if deemed necessary, admitted to a mental health unit associated with the hospital.

Most public and private hospitals have different wards for different people and conditions. This may include single-gender wards, wards for specific diagnoses, wards for different age groups and, most commonly, wards separated between 'high dependency' and 'low dependency'. The person will receive treatment over a number of days and be discharged when they are stabilised on medication, with a continuing treatment plan if needed.

A small number of people with acute episodes of psychosis are assessed by a psychiatrist and 'sectioned' or 'scheduled' under relevant state mental health legislation. This means the person is held involuntarily in hospital and cannot leave hospital because they are a threat to themselves or others.

Involuntary treatment only occurs in public hospitals. This means that acute mental health units in public hospitals are locked units, with controlled entry and exit. Locked units provide a safe place for a person who may harm themselves or others.

A typical journey for the involuntary treatment of acute psychosis in large hospitals involves starting briefly in the emergency department and then going to an acute section and then high dependency and then low dependency and then discharge to treatment in the community.

Being held involuntarily in a locked ward is a shock. You are now not only suffering from your illness but also locked in a strange place with frightening people, and you may not be able to leave. Staff are busy; access to doctors and other professionals is limited because everyone is busy. You will feel frightened, overwhelmed and confused.

You need to familiarise yourself with your environment. You need to understand the routine and rules of the ward – meal times, amenities and activities. Staff should explain all this to you, but often you need to ask them for specific information. The sooner you can get into the routine, the better you should feel about being there. Nurses are often very busy with paperwork and often lock themselves in a nursing area and ignore patients. It will be tempting to bang loudly on the door/window, and this does often get the attention of a nurse, but they may be hostile towards you or claim you are aggressive, which can lead to being taken to a more acute ward, being isolated or having your leave taken away. You will soon find nurses whom you click better with to help you and talk with for longer.

Try to make your room or personal space your own safe place with your own personal belongings. In a locked ward, some of your personal items may have been removed, and other items may not be allowed; however, you can ask your family to bring in photos that give you pleasure to go up on your wall, music that you enjoy etc.

TV, music, and books are generally available in hospital and provide distractions and relaxation and a sense of normality. However, be careful that they don't feed your delusions and hallucinations. If there is a TV in a common area, you may hear things on the TV that aren't what is actually coming out of the TV. Sometimes you can stay in your room to avoid this. It makes sense to stay away from people who confuse or disturb you, but isolating yourself is only a good idea if other stimuli become too troubling. Otherwise, it's probably better to participate in activities that are provided for patients, such as board games or physical activities if they are available. This makes you feel more 'normal' and is a distraction from what you're going through. It may also be helpful to do activities with your support persons when they visit. You are all going through a very difficult event together; doing an activity together is a safe, fun distraction that makes you all feel a little better.

Talk with staff. They are there to help but may also write down some things you say, so be open, but don't let something be misinterpreted on your file later. Try to join in activities. Talk with patients about safe topics, like their normal interests and hobbies. You may find patients you can relate to, and you can work together to help one another. You need to remember that everyone there is also traumatised. Some may become aggressive because of their condition or just because they are angry about being in a locked ward. Others may share their story with you, and this may traumatise you. Some may also confuse you with their own delusions and hallucinations or speak in unusual ways which you may misinterpret. People hospitalised for depression and anxiety may not understand psychosis, and even though they are acutely unwell like you, they may still stigmatise psychosis.

Student nurses are a great resource if they are available. They generally have more time to talk and are easier to relate to. There is likely to also be peer workers, who have experienced mental health issues before but are now employed with the hospital or volunteer their time. Ask peer workers about the rules of the hospital and the coping strategies they used when they were in acute stages of illness. You can also talk with official visitors, who may be called advocates or community visitors in some states. These people help mostly with complaints.

Private hospitals and clinics

Private hospitals or clinics are an option for voluntary admission to a hospital. Private hospitals are generally set in nice grounds with reasonable rooms (usually private but sometimes shared). You can be referred to a private hospital by a GP or psychiatrist. To get into a private hospital, you need to reassure the hospital that you are not at risk of harming yourself, are not in any legal trouble, are prepared to follow their rules and recommended therapies and voluntarily want to be there.

Private hospitals are expensive. If you have private health insurance, you need to check that your policy covers private health insurance. If you are not covered by your private health insurance provider or don't have private health insurance, check the waiting period for coverage for private hospitals. According to the commonwealth ombudsman (2017), 'psychiatric services and rehabilitation only require a two-month waiting period, even if the condition is pre-existing. This means you can be covered two months after commencing a policy'.

Northside Group (2018) also notes that commonwealth government reforms starting in April 2018 now allow eligible consumers an instant policy upgrade to cover a private psychiatric hospital admission without serving a waiting period as long as you have already served your two-month waiting period on lower cover policies. It is therefore sensible to upgrade private hospital health insurance coverage when the first signs of potential psychosis arise or during your first admission to a public hospital if you think you might need further support after discharge. Private health insurance generally covers privately run day programs like therapy and support groups (outpatient groups). You need to check this with your private health insurance provider.

Having your support persons scope out potential private hospitals might seem like a good idea, especially if you are stuck in a public hospital, but you can better demonstrate your voluntary commitment to treatment by making your own calls to admissions teams. They often have waiting lists of several weeks, so act early. Check out the rules and treatments of each hospital or clinic before making enquiries. Remember not to focus on the images of the facilities as a basis for your decision; it is really the quality of the treatment staff that matters most.

Holistic approach to treatment

The symptoms of psychosis vary from person to person. They may vary at different stages of episodes and in different episodes. Episodes of psychosis generally impact all aspects of your life, including physical, psychological and social aspects. They may also impact on everything that you do, whether it be activities in your daily life, being able to get up in the morning, personal hygiene, cooking, housework, shopping, managing your finances, going to school, uni or work, going out with other people or participating in recreational, sporting or entertainment activities.

The first priority of treatment is to treat and alleviate your symptoms as quickly as possible so that you are stabilised. You can start planning treatment for the broader aspects of your life in the acute phase, but this journey will continue through an extended recovery period.

To address not only the alleviation of your symptoms but also the broad reaching impact of an acute episode of psychosis, your treatment needs to include all the following components:

- Assessment, diagnosis and treatment plan established
- Medication to reduce your symptoms
- Case management to coordinate all aspects of your treatment and ensure continuity of care (such as GP or community mental health worker)
- Psychological support
- Therapy
- Practical support for activities of daily life, such as budgeting, self-care, housekeeping, cooking, laundry, transport, shopping (occupational therapist)
- Assistance with accommodation, financial support etc from a social worker
- Family support and support for family and friends
- Counselling, which may include help with relationships, vocational support etc
- Education about your illness
- General health support that may include programs to help with exercise, recreational activities, managing school/uni or work, managing stress, weight reduction and fitness
- Support groups

Getting the professional help you need in hospital

Hospitalisation gives you access to a range of health professionals who can help you with the treatment you need, depending on your needs. Bearing in mind that you are only likely to be in hospital for a short time, it is important that you work with your psychiatrist to identify the help you need and book in with the health professionals who can help you. You may need your support persons to advocate for you to get appointments with the professionals you need. You can talk to your psychiatrist and psychologist about your condition and work out a plan for your discharge and continuing care after discharge.

Some of the main professionals in a support network are shown in the diagram below. The professionals you work with will depend on your specific needs. Ideally, your case manager will coordinate the whole team.

Meeting the costs of treatmentFor mental illnesses that impair your ability to work or do everyday tasks and have a permanent impact, you may be able to access the National Disability Insurance Scheme (NDIS). Private and public community services can advise you on the NDIS, which may lead to an individual support package to fund services like goal setting and planning, education and training, finding employment and social or cultural activities. If you can't get on the NDIS, you may still be able to get a case manager to help you. As mentioned above, case managers are available when you are discharged from hospital to a community mental health team. However, case managers are not provided to everyone, so you may need to demonstrate your need for one or make sure your GP is coordinating all your support professionals for you.

Getting back to work, school or university can be very difficult because psychosis can cause a lack of motivation. Get inspired by reading or listening to other stories of recovery from autobiographies, support groups or resources on the web. If you find it difficult to get out of bed or the shower or look for jobs, it is probably not because you are lazy – it is because of your illness.

Meeting privacy and confidentiality requirements of information

Information that you provide to medical and health professionals is confidential. It is a good idea to talk to each of your medical and health professional team members about the privacy and confidentiality of your information. Some of your information may need to be shared with members of your health professional team. Each member of the team will discuss with you information that may be shared with other members of the team.

Health records are confidential. There are both legal and ethical requirements for health professionals to respect the privacy and confidentiality of health records. There are exceptions to this principle, such as in the event of a court case, when relevant health records may be subpoenaed through the court process. Failure to keep health records confidential may be a breach of confidentiality. It may also be a breach of specific privacy laws.

If you think a healthcare professional has breached the confidentiality of your health records or of any discussions you have had with them as part of your treatment and care, you can complain to the Health Care Complaints Commission in your state or territory.

Medication

The first priority in an acute episode is to diagnose the condition and start medication to alleviate symptoms and stabilise the condition. Medications are prescribed by a psychiatrist on the basis of the diagnosis of the condition and the symptoms the person is presenting with. There are several types of medications for mental illness. These include the following:

- Antipsychotics to treat symptoms of psychosis
- Mood stabilisers (such as for bipolar disorder)
- Antidepressants, which may be used when there are symptoms of depression
- Anti-anxiety medications when there are symptoms of anxiety

Medication is generally prescribed in tablet form or by injection. Medications may not work for some people and may work better for others. Medications may have adverse side effects. The side effects may differ from person to person. Dosage may vary over time and as the condition progresses or resolves. You need to be monitored closely when you start your medication. You need to discuss any side effects with your doctor. It is important to take your medication. You should be aware of the medications you are taking and the dosage. You should know what types of medication you are taking as you may be on more than one drug in the same category. Knowing your medications and the dosage also means that you can educate yourself about the drug and the possible side effects so you know if you are having a side effect, and you can also try to manage some of the side effects, such as weight gain.

Changes in medication may lead to a period of instability and higher risk of relapse. Discontinuing your medication without advice from a doctor is tempting but extremely dangerous. Feeling better is not a good reason to stop medication as you may still have a high risk of relapse. Side effects are another reason you might want to stop medication, but it is better to ask for alternative medications or request a reduced dose. Don't change your medication or alter doses without consulting a doctor. Forgetting medication is also common, so set reminders or get your support person to remind you.

Antipsychotic medication

During acute stages of a psychotic disorder, you will probably be given an antipsychotic. There are side effects to antipsychotics, but the risk of another psychotic episode is usually more serious than the side effects. Antipsychotics adjust the chemicals in your brain, such as dopamine, which is the chemical that influences emotions, motivation and movements. It is still unclear exactly how dopamine relates to psychosis, but there is some evidence that increased dopamine may cause psychotic symptoms. Antipsychotic medication is not a cure; it just reduces the likelihood of psychotic symptoms. Antipsychotics can reduce delusions and hallucinations in just a few days, but it can take six weeks for antipsychotics to start working properly and even longer sometimes to have their full effect.

Antipsychotics can be divided into typical antipsychotics and atypical antipsychotics. You should consult at least one psychiatrist about different medications for psychosis and ask about the side effects. If you are hospitalised or join a support group, you might also like to talk to other people who experience psychosis about their experience of medications, but remember that they work differently on different people.

A list of commonly prescribed typical and atypical antipsychotic medications follows (adapted from the drug utilisation subcommittee of the Pharmaceutical Benefits Scheme, 2016). The list may help you to gain an understanding of the medications you are taking.

Typical antipsychotics

Product	Brand name and sponsor	Notes
Chlorpromazine	Largactil (Sanofi-Aventis Australia P/L)	Oral or intramuscular injection.
Flupenthixol	Fluanxol Concentrated Depot (Lundbeck Australia P/L) Fluanxol Depot (Lundbeck Australia P/L)	Intramuscular injection.

Fluphenazine	Modecate (Bristol-Myers Squibb Australia P/L)	Intramuscular injection. When administered as maintenance therapy, a single injection may control schizophrenic symptoms up to four weeks or longer.
Haloperidol	Haldol Decanoate (Janssen-Cilag P/L) Serenace (Aspen Pharma Pty Ltd)	Intramuscular injection or oral.
Pericyazine	Neulactil (Sanofi-Aventis Australia P/L)	Oral.
Trifluoperazine	Stelazine [Amdipharm Mercury (Australia) P/L]	Oral.
Zuclopenthixol	Clopixol Depot (Lundbeck Australia P/L)	Intramuscular injection.

Atypical antipsychotics

Product	Brand name and sponsor	Notes
Amisulpride	Several generic brands Solian (Sanofi-Aventis Australia P/L)	For acute psychotic episodes.
Aripiprazole	Abilify (Otsuka Australia Pharmaceutical P/L) Abilify Maintena (Lundbeck Australia P/L)	Used for both schizophrenia and bipolar.
Asenapine	Saphris (Lundbeck Australia P/L)	Used for both schizophrenia and bipolar.
Clozapine	Clopine (Hospira P/L) Clopine Suspension (Hospira P/L) Clozaril (Novartis Pharmaceuticals Australia P/L)	'Clozapine is the most effective antipsychotic but is reserved for people with schizophrenia who have not adequately responded to two other antipsychotics. It has a high adverse event burden and requires close monitoring' (Winckel and Siskind, 2017).
Lurasidone	Latuda [Servier Laboratories (Australia) P/L]	Used for schizophrenia.
Olanzapine	Several generic brands Zyprexa (Eli Lilly Australia P/L)	Used in schizophrenia and related disorders as well for acute mania in bipolar.

Paliperidone	Invega (Janssen-Cilag P/L) Invega Sustenna (Janssen-Cilag P/L)	Used in schizophrenia and schizoaffective disorder orally or with injection.
Quetiapine	Several generic brands Seroquel (AstraZeneca P/L)	Used in bipolar for both depression and acute mania. Also used in schizophrenia.
Risperidone	Several generic brands Risperdal (Janssen-Cilag P/L)	For schizophrenia and bipolar mania.
Ziprasidone	APO-Ziprasidone (Apotex P/L) Zeldox (Pfizer Australia P/L)	For schizophrenia and bipolar mania.

Changing medication

Antipsychotics may not work initially or may cause adverse side effects. New medications are being trialled. Adverse side effects from antipsychotics listed by the U.S. National Institute of Mental Health (2018) include the following:

- Drowsiness
- Dizziness
- Restlessness
- Weight gain (the risk is higher with some atypical antipsychotic medicines)
- Dry mouth
- Constipation
- Nausea
- Vomiting
- Blurred vision
- Low blood pressure
- Uncontrollable movements, such as tics and tremors (the risk is higher with typical antipsychotic medicines)
- Seizures
- Low white blood cell count, making it harder to fight infections

It's important to research the specific side effects of your medication and the likelihood of each side effect so that you are aware in the event of your experiencing any of them. Side effects generally only occur in a small number of people, and they may differ from person to person. Remember that your doctor will weigh up the side effects with the risk of a relapse into psychosis. Your doctor is the best judge of the comparative risks to your physical and mental health. Even so, you have the right to decide what medication you take unless you are subject to involuntary hospital admission or a community treatment order. For most people though, you have some say in what medications you take. Private psychiatrists tend to be more flexible in allowing you to have some input about the medications you take.

Psychiatrists may also differ in their diagnosis of your condition and therefore which drugs they prescribe for you. Their diagnosis and choice of drugs is based on their interpretation of diagnostic information, what you tell them about your symptoms, the stage of psychosis you are at when you see them, changes in the duration and frequency of psychotic episodes and the expertise and experience of the psychiatrist. Changes in diagnosis can be troubling, especially if you go from something like depression to bipolar or bipolar to schizophrenia as these changes seem like you have more serious illnesses. It is important to remember that your diagnosis forms the basis for the medication you are prescribed to treat your symptoms and return you to good health.

In recovery stages, you may be prescribed different antipsychotics. If you have a mood disorder, causing psychosis like bipolar disorder, you will probably be prescribed a mood stabiliser – like lithium or Epilim, which could prevent psychosis by itself or could be given to you in combination with an antipsychotic – and, in some cases, also antidepressants or antianxiety medication.

Medications may be very expensive, even though most of them are subsidised through the Pharmaceutical Benefits Scheme. If you have a diagnosis such as a major depressive or bipolar disorder, it might also cost you more for certain antipsychotic medication because only people with schizophrenia get the full subsidy through a special script known as a PBS/RPBS Authority prescription.

Developing an emergency management plan (EMP)

It is a good idea to record all the important information on your condition and compile it into an emergency management plan (EMP) on a single page. Information in an EMP includes the following:

- Medical team (such as GP, psychiatrist, psychologist) and their contact details
- Preferred hospitals (such as private hospital, local public hospital emergency department) and their contact details
- Carers/support persons with their mobile contacts
- Early warning signs of psychosis (mild signs and signs of acute episode)
- Usual medications and dosage (important as your medications and dosage may change frequently)
- Emergency medications for acute symptoms (this may be a stronger antipsychotic or a higher dose of your current medication and may be the difference between a bad day and a relapse)

You can carry the EMP with you so you have details of your medical contacts, medications, contact persons, early warning signs etc and can share them as needed. You can, for example, refer to your EMP if your GP (or other professionals) ask you what medications you're on or what psychologist you're seeing. You can share your EMP with your support persons so they also have your medical information. Recording early warning signs in your EMP is helpful, so your support persons appreciate signs and symptoms that may signal changes that need to be discussed and potentially addressed. This may be particularly helpful for support persons as they can draw your attention to examples that demonstrate that you may currently have early warning signs of psychosis. The discussion can then focus on the action that needs to be taken to address the changes. Actions may include going with the person to their GP, making an appointment with their psychiatrist, presenting at the emergency department of the hospital or arranging an admission to a private hospital.

Sample emergency management plan template

To download a copy of this EMP, go to madnarrative.org/emp.

Name: DOB: / /   Most recent diagnoses: Preferred helpline/crisis number:

Medical team		
GP Address: Ph:	Psychiatrist Address: Ph:	Psychologist/Case worker Address: Ph:
Hospitals		
Preferred clinic (if they have a bed) Address: Ph:	If near home Address: Ph:	If near work Address: Ph:
Carers/Support persons		
Primary carer Mob:	Secondary carer Mob:	Additional support person Mob:
Early warning signs (EWS)		
Early signs	Mild signs	Signs of acute episode
Plans of action after noticing EWS (Plans/Treatment/Meds)		
Usual medications	PRNs for acute symptoms	Effective self-soothing and self-care strategies

Therapy

Types of therapies

Therapy has a role in the lead-up to psychosis and in the recovery stages but can be of limited use in acute stages. When you are experiencing an acute psychotic episode, it can be difficult to understand therapists and hard to express the many confusing feelings and thoughts experienced. You might also fail to trust therapists or become suspicious of their questions. During the acute phase, particularly when you are hospitalised, you may take the opportunity to work with your psychiatrist and psychologist to try to determine your goals for recovery and understand the types of therapies that are available that may help you to achieve your goals.

Even though therapy may be difficult in the acute phase, it is likely to be beneficial and a part of your treatment plan once you have stabilised your condition and are on the road to recovery. Regular therapy is important for most people to stay well. This may involve psychiatrists who mostly focus on medication, psychologists who offer therapy to address negative thoughts and behaviours or counsellors to address trauma that may have led to psychosis.

Therapists can become very expensive, unless you are a public patient, when it is generally free. However, as a public patient, you may only get appointments with psychiatrists every three months or even less frequently, which might not be often enough if you need regular monitoring of medication and symptoms.

Overall, therapy should involve at least the following five elements (see Mental Health in Australia, 2012):

1. **Coping with distressing symptoms** — Shouting at voices in your head or drowning them out with loud music can be effective but can also make things worse. The therapist should recommend coping strategies based on evidence and the experience of other clients.
2. **Modifying delusions and other beliefs** — Though you cannot rationalise with delusions, they can be modified by giving alternative explanations for things and offering evidence that you can use to question delusions. With delusions, you should try to check the facts. Weird coincidences tend to happen when you behave in new ways, and sometimes your delusions are based on a shred of evidence. A technique in cognitive behaviour therapy (CBT) and DBT is to write down the hard facts and your interpretations of those facts. Then think of alternative explanations for the facts to

check if your interpretations are unlikely. Even the things that have a 0.0001 per cent probability or less can seem like they are true when you experience psychosis. Share these facts, interpretations and alternative explanations with someone you trust to see if you have delusions. If you have auditory hallucinations that instruct you to act in a particular way, this is known as a 'command hallucination', and there is a specific branch of CBT that may be effective for you called cognitive therapy for command hallucinations (CTCH).

3. **Understanding what has happened to you** — This includes general knowledge about the illness and its causes but, more importantly, includes individualised knowledge of how symptoms developed. Developing a narrative around what happened is important, but then you must try to create a new narrative about recovery and renewal.

4. **Building a stronger self** — Try to take on new meaningful roles and forge new friendships. CBT can help you combat negative beliefs about yourself.

5. **Living more fully and minimising relapse** — Use therapy to overcome negative emotions and address symptoms so you can return to a more fulfilling life.

Some of the more common therapies that you may consider include the following:

- Cognitive behaviour therapy (CBT)
- Dialectical behaviour therapy (DBT)
- Psychoeducation
- Mindfulness
- Open dialogue
- Acceptance and commitment therapy
- Befriending therapy
- Family therapy
- Music therapy and art therapy

Cognitive behaviour therapy (CBT) can help you to identify the source of a delusional belief and then challenge that belief.

Dialectical behaviour therapy (DBT) is a variation of CBT that can help you tolerate distress, regulate emotions and improve interpersonal relationships. These may not eliminate psychosis but may help you avoid the triggers of a future psychotic episode.

Psychoeducation helps you learn about your illness and ways to treat it. However, processing this information may be difficult if you have delusions, hallucinations or disorganised thinking. During an acute psychotic episode, it may be better to seek out simple explanations or stories from peers who have experienced psychosis. Psychoeducation is also very important for carers and other support people as it helps them understand more about the illness and its treatment.

Mindfulness is increasingly trendy in self-help circles and is found in some variants of CBT. Mindfulness is also a significant component of DBT. Many people are resistant to mindfulness or get a very generic introduction to it, which can turn you off. There is some evidence though that it can be helpful in reducing the symptoms of psychosis. There are many free recordings on the web for mindfulness-based stress reduction, but there are also psychosis-specific mindfulness practices. Mindfulness can help with relaxation, but that is not the goal. The goal of mindfulness is to pay attention to the present moment and is not about stopping thoughts like in some forms of meditation. Some basics of mindfulness involve the following:

- Become aware of in-breaths, the slight pause between breaths and out-breaths.
- Focus on parts of your body and what you are feeling inside.
- Acknowledge thoughts that arise and do not judge or oppose those thoughts.
- Try to detach yourself from a hallucination and just observe it without engaging it.
- Reflect on your values, purpose in life and what's important to you.
- Identify your goals and don't act on thoughts that go against these goals.
- Accept that you may have negative thoughts but that these will pass.
- Remember that thoughts do not have to control your behaviour.

Open dialogue is a less common treatment but is starting to show results for people with psychosis. Open dialogue is an approach developed in Finland involving your whole family. There are seven principles of open dialogue, which are good principles for other treatment options (Bergström et al, 2017):

1. Get immediate help — Prevent hospitalisation, if possible, by acting within twenty-four hours from first contact.
2. Activate social network — Involve members of your social network in the first meeting to get support for you and your family.
3. Flexibility and mobility — Therapy is tailored to your specific needs, and there are integrative therapeutic methods.
4. Responsibility — The first person contacted organises the first meeting, where further decisions on treatment are made.
5. Psychological continuity — The initial team remains responsible during all treatments.
6. Tolerance of uncertainty — Early conclusions are to be avoided, and no antipsychotics should be prescribed at the first meeting, but more meetings should follow soon after the first meeting.
7. Dialogism — Create an equal dialogue among consumers, the support network and treatment staff.

Acceptance and commitment therapy (ACT) helps you to accept your symptoms and can make delusions less believable. ACT may involve simply noticing thoughts and not trying to determine whether they are true or false. ACT can also help to change your behaviours reacting to hallucinations, delusions and negative thoughts. ACT may also be useful in depression, which often occurs following an acute episode of psychosis (Gumley et al, 2015). In ACT and also in narrative therapy, there is often the use of metaphors. Simple metaphors can be very effective, but sometimes when you experience psychosis, metaphors can seem like someone is talking in a strange code and you looking for hidden meaning in what they are saying. If this is the case, ask your therapist what they mean in plain English or request the narrative therapy approach of creating your own metaphors to describe what you are experiencing.

Befriending therapy is a lesser known option for reducing symptoms of psychosis. It involves social support to combat isolation by having someone listen carefully to you and offering practical support (*Befriending Manual*, 2003). If you have paranoia, this might not be the best treatment unless you fully trust the person and do not become suspicious of their intentions. Befriending therapy may also involve activities like walks and games. The companionship may seem forced, but many who volunteer are also seeking new friends, so the relationship can sometimes become genuine.

Family therapy is another option and involves bringing members of your family together to reduce triggers of stress and work together to treat psychosis. Narrative therapy is popular within family therapy and involves seeing psychosis as separate from you as a person. Family therapy, like many other forms of therapy, may require ten or more sessions to be effective.

Music therapy and art therapy may also help reduce the symptoms of psychosis. These can be done with professionals, or you can listen to your own music and create your own art. With music, choose calming songs that remind you of good points in your life and reflect on what the lyrics mean to you and how they make you feel. With art, don't worry about making good art; just express your emotions with drawing, painting or sculpting clay. You might also work with digital media, like photography and audio recordings, to document what you are experiencing.

You may also look for alternative therapies such as reiki healing or Chinese herbal medicine. Be careful with these treatments because people may tell you it worked for them, but scientific evidence usually does not support their use. Some herbs can also interact badly with your other medications, so tell your doctors before you take them. There are also nutritional therapies which can improve mental health by increasing your intake of vitamins, minerals or omega 3 fatty acid. Again, often these are sometimes not backed by substantial evidence, so be careful not to waste your money and do not substitute any alternative treatments for your normal medication.

Selecting the best therapy for you

As you can see, there are a lot of therapeutic treatment options. Your health professional team can help you determine which therapies best suit your current needs and situation. They can help you work out your priorities and the therapy options that best meet those options. You may also need different therapies at different stages of your treatment.

It is also a good idea to read up on therapies that may meet your needs and talk with others with similar conditions either through support groups or online and ask them what has worked for them. It is also helpful to get some feedback to find the right therapist. If therapy doesn't seem to be working for you, you might not need a different type of therapy, just a different therapist whom you get along with better. If you live in a regional or remote area and don't have access to many local therapists, consider telehealth, where you phone or Skype with a therapist.

Discharge from hospital

The length of stay in a public hospital is generally relatively short. Once you are stabilised on medication, relatively free from symptoms and interacting in hospital with others, the psychiatrist will generally hold a family meeting and discuss a trial night at home. If this trial is successful, the psychiatrist is likely to discharge you from hospital.

If a person is at risk of hurting themselves or others, they may be held involuntarily in a locked ward in a mental health unit. The requirements for detaining a person involuntarily are legislated to ensure patients are only detained involuntarily (that is, they are scheduled) if they meet the strict conditions set out in the legislation. For this reason, they can only be discharged with authorisation from the hospital psychiatrist, or they may have to be cleared through a mental health review tribunal. Mental illness is covered under state legislation, so you need to check out the law in your state or territory.

Though each state and territory in Australia differs in its legislation on involuntary treatment, all have some form of mental health review tribunal (Barnett, 2012). Tribunals are most often used during compulsory hospital admissions to determine whether a less restrictive form of care is appropriate. They may also decide on issues such as transfers to other states or territories, electroconvulsive therapy (ECT), appeals and other matters that vary between states and territories.

If you are scheduled (detained involuntarily) in a mental health unit, you will generally be assigned a lawyer free of charge from Legal Aid who can give you advice about tribunals. Legal Aid lawyers tend to be much more experienced in tribunals than other lawyers whom you may be tempted to contact because they have helped you with previous matters. Your lawyer should meet you at least a day before the tribunal and explain to you the following:

- The tribunal process
- What powers the tribunals have and what decisions they can make for you
- What to say and what not to say
- Different types of evidence that you can give, such as written and oral evidence before, during or after the hearing

Planning your treatment in the community

To continue your pathway to recovery and to prevent relapse, you need a comprehensive continuing treatment plan that begins when you are discharged from hospital. Most hospitals help you plan for discharge.

The continuing treatment needs to include the following:

- A GP whom you trust and can form an ongoing relationship with
- A case manager who coordinates all your treatment (such as your GP or psychologist)
- A psychiatrist who will continue to see you on an ongoing basis to monitor your symptoms, medication and treatment
- A psychologist who helps you to adjust to your condition and manage any aspects of your life that may be a challenge

You may also engage with other professionals as appropriate to your needs such as the following:

- A dietician to help address weight gain (which may be a side effect of antipsychotic medication)
- A social worker to help with applying for government financial assistance or finding accommodation

- An occupational therapist for assistance with activities of daily living or adjustments to studies or work or planning

You should also find out about the services offered by community mental health teams, therapy options and support groups. It is a good idea to join therapy and support groups to support you through your period of recovery and adjustment to your condition and to prevent recurrence.

Support persons' role in an acute episode

The first priority for a support person during an acute episode is to get urgent medical treatment for the person in whatever form is appropriate. Ideally, you can have a discussion about where to present for treatment, considering that the location you choose is likely to be where you are admitted for treatment. For example, if the person is seriously ill, they may need to present to the emergency department of a local public hospital for assessment. The person may then be admitted to the public mental health unit at that hospital.

If you recognise your symptoms but feel you need admission to a hospital for treatment, you may be able to book into your GP for a referral to a private hospital. You or your support person can then phone the private hospital to check whether you meet the criteria for admission and they have availability for admission. You may also be admitted to a private hospital for other reasons, such as adjustments to your medications.

If there is immediate danger presented to the person experiencing psychosis or to others, then you must call emergency services on 000. In less extreme cases, call a mental health line in your state or territory (see the Resources section for the crisis numbers). Where available, they may put you through to a mental health crisis team in the area where you live. Try to keep the person you care for involved in the process of getting help for them. The mental health crisis team can conduct a home visit and work with you and your support person(s) to decide what actions need to be taken. Where needed, the mental health crisis team can accompany you to the local hospital for assessment and possible admission.

The problem with getting help for a person with an acute psychotic episode may be that they have no insight into how seriously ill they are. This means that they may refuse to seek treatment for their condition, refuse to meet with the mental health crisis team and refuse to give consent for you to seek help on their behalf. In this case, as a support person or persons, you need to assess whether they are a threat to harming themselves or others. If you think they are in danger of harming themselves or others, then you can call the mental health crisis team or the police depending on the urgency. The mental health crisis team can conduct a home visit, assess action needed and escort you to hospital if required. The mental health crisis teams may be accompanied by police officers, which may alarm someone with psychosis but may be necessary to diffuse difficult situations.

What to do when the person you care for tells you they're being ruled by aliens

Knowing what to do for the symptoms of psychosis is very hard because you don't know what to say or do. It must be terrifying to hear voices or feel that you're being ruled by aliens. What do you say when someone tells you this? There isn't a right or wrong thing to say, but there are some helpful guidelines:

- Don't take anything that they say personally. They are ill.
- Listen to what they're telling you as it's very real to them, and it may help them to tell you about it. Respond with sympathy, like 'That must be very frightening'.
- Don't go along with their delusions but also resist temptations to try and correct delusions because this may actually lead to a stronger belief in delusions or may foster mistrust in you.
- Avoid confrontations and criticism.
- Try to find things to talk about that are neutral or simple things that you can do together, like going for a short walk.

Supporting a person in hospital

If the person you care for is admitted to hospital, you need to take an active role in their care rather than think that the hospital will look after everything. It may be appropriate to visit often or just to call, depending on what the person you care for wants. If you trigger certain emotions or thoughts, try not to blame yourself – blame the illness. Sometimes, if you are a trigger, you need to stay away completely, which can be difficult, but there are still other ways to help. Check what is prohibited and what is allowed in the hospital and drop in appropriate items. This may include the following:

- Shoes without shoelaces as these may be prohibited
- Pants or skirts that are held up with elastic (drawstrings and belts may be prohibited)
- Photos of pets and loved ones plus Blu Tack if permitted
- A music player with cordless rechargeable headphones or a wireless speaker (cords, music players with glass or cameras, charging cords and batteries may not be allowed)
- Individually wrapped chocolates or lollies that can be shared with other patients and staff
- Decaffeinated and low-sugar drinks in plastic bottles (caffeinated drinks, glass bottles and metal cans may be prohibited)
- Pyjamas, but these might not be permitted to be worn outside a room
- Medications or alternative therapies, which will need to be left with the nurses
- Toiletries (mouthwash should be alcohol-free, and deodorant should not be an aerosol)

You may also need to advocate on behalf of the person you care about. They may not be seeing their doctor frequently enough or may need access to other professionals, like social workers (who can help with financial support or accommodation on discharge), dieticians (who can help manage weight gain from antipsychotics), exercise physiologists (who help keep the person active) and occupational therapists (who help with coping strategies and discharge planning). If you feel a doctor is failing to authorise a discharge at an appropriate time, you do have a right to have this opinion heard and should politely but assertively act on this right to advocate on behalf of the person you care about.

You may also need to offer practical support during and after a hospitalisation. This may include paying bills, informing work, school or university about sick days (being careful to only disclose the absolute minimum) and scheduling and accompanying the person you care for to medical appointments where appropriate.

Look after yourself

As well as caring for others, you need to care for yourself. Experiencing a psychotic episode is distressing not only for the person you care for but also for their support persons. Don't put your own physical or mental well-being at risk. Consider seeking counselling yourself for support and to help you work through some of the situations that may arise from time to time. You may be eligible for financial support for counselling. Your GP may be able to give you a mental health plan that subsidises counselling sessions. You may also need to ask the person you care for to nominate additional carers or support people as respite.

Carer vignette — A mum's experience of getting treatment for an acute episode

Mark's partner, Ray, and I were trying to cope with Mark's first psychotic episode. He couldn't sleep. He was in a frenzy of activity all night. He was angry about the way he'd been treated at work and was firing off emails to his current and former employers, the ABC and other journalists. He was agitated and irritable, particularly with Ray and me. He was on the move night and day. He didn't appear to know how bad he was. I felt frightened for him, overwhelmingly sad and powerless to help him. I was relieved to make contact with the local community mental health team. They also spoke with Ray. We explained what was happening. They said they'd visit him at 11:00 a.m. That morning, I awoke to perhaps fifty text messages from Mark that didn't make any sense. I raced to his apartment. His brother Paul had also received the text messages and was there. I didn't go into the apartment because my presence angered Mark. Paul went in. We were worried about Ray's safety. The mental health team arrived at eleven with the police. That was the saddest day of my life, watching six burly policeman kitted up in their riot gear to 'help' my very ill son. It was with tremendous relief that Mark went with them willingly and was scheduled into an acute mental health unit. I visited him at the ward. He was deeply traumatised by being held down by a security guard, having his pants removed and being given an injection. He took me by the hand into the toilet. He was under the control of blue lights. We sat on the floor together, and he pressed the buzzer on and off. He was terrified. I just sat there with him.

Don't let this scenario happen to you or your loved ones. Recognise and act on symptoms early. My feeling is that you go with your instincts. If you feel your loved one is behaving vastly differently from normal, talk to them and ask them to go to hospital with you. Let the experts assess them.

Carer vignette — A partner's experience of getting treatment for an acute episode

I did not understand mental illness much at all, especially not mania and psychosis. The talk of the cameras was unusual and troubling. The real stress of his work only became clear after Mark sent me emails he had sent to a lawyer. We tried to de-stress by going to the Blue Mountains for a night. On the way, Mark insisted we get off at Redfern Station – the station closest to Sydney Uni. He recounted his feeling of suicidal intent, waiting on the platform and holding a post so he didn't throw himself in front of the train. If you ever feel this way, call Lifeline on 13 11 14 or get to a hospital straight away.

On the journey to the hotel in Leura, he explained more about work but used unusual metaphors like a jigsaw puzzle and kept changing topics. He couldn't sleep. The next day, we got the train home, and he continued talking about puzzles and then also about signs and coincidences. He had a panic attack, and we had to get off the train in the middle of nowhere. Then he quickly oscillated between crying and laughing. On the platform, he again talked about the cameras and said he would get compensation from Sydney Uni.

We got back to Sydney and later went to a friend's house for dinner. The friend had experienced psychosis before and so helped explain to me what it's like. We decided we needed to get Mark to hospital, but he wouldn't go. We involved Mark's mum, who eventually called the mental health line, and their crisis team unfortunately involved police, who nearly broke down our door. For the first few nights in hospital, Mark was much sicker than before, and many of the people in there were very scary.

Pathways to recovery

*The roads to wellness are many and varied. For many of us,
the recovery journey stretches over many years. Change comes
over time with persistence, quality treatment and a supportive
community of family, friends and work colleagues.*

— Jack Heath, CEO, SANE, 2018

Focusing on a holistic wellness approach to recovery

Some people have a short episode of psychosis, see a doctor, take their
medications, get over the episode and recover completely. However, recovery
may not necessarily mean a cure. It is estimated that roughly one-third of
persons experiencing a psychotic episode will have only that one single
episode, one-third will have several episodes with minimal impairment
and one-third will have several episodes and residual impairment.

Many conditions will be lifelong, and medications may need to continue for
the rest of your life. Medication aims to stabilise the condition so that you can
lead a normal life. It also aims to prevent relapse. The most likely continuing
medication is antipsychotic medication. This may be as a tablet or injection.
Injections involve a system of slow release of medication, which can be useful
if you often forget to take your tablets. You can also be legally forced to have
regular injections (through a community treatment order). Taking medication
for the rest of your life may be difficult to accept, especially considering the
side effects of the long-term use of antipsychotics and mood stabilisers.

To make the most from this situation and achieve the best possible
outcomes, it is important for you to build your life into a healthy pattern

of physical and psychological wellness, with a strong support group and social network of friends and a rewarding array of activities that you participate in that may include studies, work, recreation, sports, hobbies and entertainment. By so doing, you have positioned yourself to be able to cope with the challenges life inevitably throws at you, identify, address and resolve any symptoms of psychosis that may arise and ward off episodes of psychosis wherever possible but cope better if they do occur.

Recovery is not only about taking medication. Recovery is about self-care – taking control of our lives and doing everything in our power to make a full recovery wherever possible and creating the best possible situation to prevent another episode. In the words of Sydney actor Annalise Braakensiek, who talked openly about her struggles with mental health, 'You need people to care and be there, but self-care is imperative as well . . . I tackle it every way I can.'

The World Health Organisation (WHO) defines mental health as 'a state of well-being in which every individual realises his or her own potential, can cope with the normal stresses of life, can work productively and fruitfully and is able to make a contribution to her or his community'. Mental health is not merely the absence of disease. Achieving 'mental health' involves actively working on all aspects of your life throughout your life to achieve a healthy and fulfilling life.

Taking a holistic approach to recovery focuses on re-establishing your life by identifying how psychosis impacts each aspect of your life – including the physical, psychological and social aspects of your life – and the impact of each area on yourself, your activities of daily life, your interactions with others and your studies, work and other activities.

CHIME — A mental framework for recovery

CHIME is a very helpful conceptual framework for recovery that fits with a holistic wellness approach to recovery. The framework provides you with a simple way of remaining positive and focused on your own personal recovery. For more details on CHIME, go to the Mind Australia website (www.mindaustralia.org.au). CHIME is an acronym for the following:

- Connectedness
  - Peer support
  - Support from others
  - Relationships
- Hope and optimism
  - Having the motivation to change
  - Having dreams and aspirations
  - A belief in the possibility of recovery
  - Positive thinking
- Identity
  - Acceptance (self and others)
  - Incorporating experiences into a positive sense of self
  - Seeing the person and not the illness
  - Self-stigma
- Meaning
  - Finding understanding of the illness
  - Spirituality
  - Meaningful activities
  - Meaningful life and social role/goals
  - Quality of life
- Empowerment
  - Having control over life
  - Personal responsibility
  - Focusing on strengths

Impacts of psychosis on wellness

The importance of taking control of your life and focusing on wellness is reflected in the scientific evidence of the impact of complex mental health conditions such as psychosis on the physical, psychological and social well-being of people who have these conditions.

General impacts of psychosis on physical health

The impact of psychosis on physical health and well-being is reflected in research demonstrating higher rates of cardiovascular and metabolic illnesses, infectious diseases, respiratory illness and substance abuse in people with psychosis.

Lifestyle factors (such as sedentary lifestyle, poor diet, high consumption of alcohol, smoking and self-medication), treatment with antipsychotics and mood stabilisers that may have significant side effects such as weight gain and liver and thyroid damage, and limited access to health services have also been reported as contributors to poorer physical health among people with psychosis (Moreno et al, 2013).

People with complex mental health conditions such as psychosis are more likely to drink, smoke and use drugs. Obesity levels are also high, contributing to greater rates of heart disease and other conditions. This is partly due to the weight gain side effects of antipsychotics.

Research also shows that people with complex mental health conditions such as psychosis have a shorter life span and increased risk of dying prematurely, with a death rate twice that of the general population and an average life expectancy twelve to fifteen years less than the general population. There is also a higher rate of suicide.

Physical and psychological health are strongly linked together. So recovery means working hard on your physical health while also working on your mental health. Seeing your GP regularly is important in addressing both physical and mental health.

General impacts of psychosis on social well-being

Experiencing a psychotic episode can be a very lonely and isolating time with disastrous and debilitating social consequences. Research shows that people with complex mental conditions have fewer and poorer social relationships (Robustelli et al, 2017). Good personal and social relationships and being part of a community are vital to maintaining good mental health and making a full recovery from psychotic episodes.

The symptoms of psychosis, the medication and its side effects all impact on the social health and well-being of sufferers. People with psychosis are trying to deal with their symptoms, which are frightening and confusing for them, and are frequently anti-social, making it difficult for them to relate to other people and, at times, frightening for people relating to them. They may isolate themselves and lack motivation, confidence and self-esteem. They may find it difficult to even get out of bed in the morning. They may find it difficult to carry out the normal activities of daily life – looking after themselves, personal hygiene, dressing, washing, laundering clothes, cooking, cleaning up their homes, managing transportation, going out, shopping etc. They may have difficulties concentrating and be unable to go to school or work. They may have financial difficulties impacting all aspects of their lives.

Activity: Identifying and planning to address the impacts of your condition on your life

1. Think about how your illness is impacting your life.
2. Consider how it may be impacting each aspect of your life, including your physical and psychological health and well-being and your relationships with others.
3. Also consider the activities that you do in your life and record how your illness may be impacting those activities.
4. Consider aspects of your daily living (cooking, housework, transport, finances, budgeting, accommodation etc), recreational and entertainment activities, your education and/or work (as appropriate).
5. Record these aspects and organise to meet with a health professional such as a psychologist, social worker or school or university counsellor to discuss these areas and work out your priorities and how you may be able to start to address them.

Planning your pathway to wellness

As discussed, episodes of psychosis generally impact all aspects of your life. Recovery from a psychotic episode focuses not only on getting over the episode but also on re-establishing your life and doing everything in your power to ensure you stay well and don't relapse. For you to have the best chance of making a full recovery, treatment needs to address each aspect of life that is impacted by the condition.

Your psychologist can help you identify aspects of your life that are impacted by your condition and help you work out your priorities and determine plans for addressing the priorities. This may include making lifestyle changes such as healthy eating, physical and recreational activities and reducing unhealthy habits such as smoking, alcohol and drugs. It is critical to maintain and build your social network and establish a range of activities that you enjoy doing. It is also important to pick up the pre-episode parts of your life and re-examine them and make adjustments accordingly. This may be a lifelong journey.

Tracking your recovery

There is a range of apps available to help you monitor your mental health and well-being status. The apps can help you monitor your progress to recovery, confirm that you are improving or help you identify early warning signs that may need to be acted on. They can also help you plan your recovery. They help you set a baseline, plan your goals and work out how to achieve them. You can share the results with your supporters and discuss your progress with them. You can also take the results with you to your appointments with health professionals such as psychologists, counsellors, social workers and occupational therapists as a basis for planning and recognising progress or dealing with setbacks.

A list of apps is included in the Resources section of this guide. Several of the popular apps are the Black Dog Institute's Snapshot, Mind Australia's How Are You Going? and Beyond Blue's Beyond Now Safety Planning.

Developing your wellness action plan

While you continue to take your medication and follow your treatment plan, working through the following material gives you other activities that you can do that help you re-establish your life, have a positive impact on your life and may help distract you from the more negative aspects of your life.

You can use the materials as a basis for discussion with your psychologist, GP, counsellor and/or other professionals as appropriate to continue your journey to wellness. They may help you to identify simple actions you can take, like medical and dental health checks. They may help you to identify your priorities and the main area you'd like to focus on, such as healthy eating to prevent weight gain. They may simply start a conversation or give you ideas about what you'd like to do and who you can go to for support to do it. We wish you well with your journey.

Improving your physical health and well-being

Goal: To be physically well and free from physical disease and in a position to function well to reach your potential in your environment.

Treatment activities: To achieve this goal, treatment activities may include looking after your general health by doing the following:

- Screening for symptoms of chronic diseases such as diabetes, raised cholesterol, heart disease, obesity, thyroid activity
- Immunisations such as flu vaccine, shingles, pneumococcal vaccine, meningococcal vaccine and the human papilloma virus (HPV) vaccine
- Dental care
- Healthy lifestyle, including healthy eating, physical activity, proper sleep and reducing unhealthy habits such as smoking, alcohol, and drugs

Improving your psychological health and well-being

Goal: To be cognitively healthy (the way we think), emotionally healthy (the way we feel) and socially healthy (have healthy relationships) so that you can reach your potential, cope with the normal stresses of life, work productively and fruitfully and make a contribution to your community.

Treatment activities: To achieve this goal, treatment activities include looking after your psychological health and well-being by doing the following:

- Working with your health professional team to develop and implement a plan to manage your illness, which includes managing your symptoms, staying well, managing any recurrences of your illness and working with your health professional team and support persons on all aspects of your treatment plan, including the following:
  - o Medication to reduce your symptoms and recover
  - o Psychological support as needed
  - o Therapy (as appropriate)
- Establishing a relationship with a health professional such as a psychologist to identify your life goals, establish priorities and endeavour to address achievable goals in your life

Improving your social health and well-being

Goal: To have good personal and social relationships so that you are not isolated, feel good about yourself, feel connected with others and feel a part of your community.

Treatment activities: To achieve this goal, treatment activities may include the following:

- Working with your health professional team to develop and implement a plan for maintaining and building your social network and establishing a range of activities that you enjoy doing
- Maintaining and building a network of family and friends whom you trust who can provide you with support and feedback and do activities with you
- Counselling and support for reinforcing healthy relationships and managing challenges with interpersonal relationships
- Joining and participating in support groups as appropriate
- Participating in online forums as appropriate
- Joining recreational, sporting or hobby groups

Addressing challenges around activities of daily living

Goal:

- To be able to manage daily living tasks such as money, self-care, housekeeping, cooking, laundry, transport and shopping.
- To have adequate accommodation and finances to be able to finance treatment and lead a reasonable life.

Activities: To achieve this goal, activities may include the following:

- Working with a social worker in regard to assistance with accommodation, financial support etc as needed
- Working with Centrelink to organise social security and other services such as income support, sickness allowance, mobility allowance, payment support for job seekers etc
- Working with an occupational therapist to develop and implement a plan for addressing challenging areas of daily living, such as shopping or managing transport
- Joining support groups focusing on cooking, budgeting etc as appropriate
- Participating in training in areas such as cooking and budgeting

Addressing challenges around recreation, education and work

Goal: To be able to achieve your full potential and make a contribution to your community.

Activities: To achieve this goal, activities may include the following:

- Working with your health professional team, such as occupational therapist and psychologist, to identify issues and challenges with your studies/work/recreational activities and developing and implementing a plan to address these
- Establishing a relationship with a health professional such as a psychologist to identify your life goals, establish priorities and endeavour to address achievable goals in your life
- Working with your health professional team to develop and implement a plan for establishing a range of activities that you enjoy doing
- Doing activities with your family and friends that you enjoy doing
- Working with your school, university or manager and HR at work to discuss your condition and identify any accommodations that need to be made, such as special assistance with assessment, extending assessment dates, working at home, revising your job description, changing your hours of work etc
- Talking to your teachers to explain your situation and request considerations such as adjusting assessment types or extending assignment deadlines
- Reducing the number of study units or going from full-time study to part-time or extending your completion dates
- Taking sick leave to recover from stressful periods
- Meeting with your supervisor at work to adjust your role (such as changing your role to work on a specific project for a period), change your job description (such as giving some of your tasks to others), assign varying working hours for a period (such as working part-time or job sharing) or make you work from home for a period
- Joining a sport, recreational or hobby group
- Joining a gym or working with a personal trainer

- Consulting a dietician or joining Weight Watchers or a similar group (as appropriate)
- Doing community education classes or a course at TAFE

Community support programs

Public community mental health centres are available in capital cities of Australia and some regional locations. When you are discharged from a mental health unit, you may be referred to the community mental health team near where you live. The teams generally comprise a psychiatrist, nurses, psychologists and other health professional groups. You are generally allocated a case manager who is your point of contact, coordinates your treatment and meets with you regularly to discuss your progress. The centres may also have day programs that may include support groups and therapy programs such as CBT.

Training

Training in recovery

Training in recovery is available in some capital cities from specialised recovery colleges. These colleges offer psychoeducation and skills development courses. Recovery colleges exist in South East Sydney, Western Sydney and Southern Adelaide, and the Mind Recovery College has eight locations in Victoria and two in South Australia. Currently, there is also planning for recovery colleges in Western Australia and Canberra, but unfortunately, the recent Canberra funding bid was unsuccessful.

There is also specific training that is useful for chronic psychosis. For example, psychotic disorders may involve cognitive impairment in terms of your speed of processing information, attention and concentration, orientation, judgement, abstraction, verbal or visual learning and working memory (ICD-11, 2018). Antipsychotic medication can improve these aspects of cognition, but each medication differs in its effectiveness in reducing cognitive impairment. Cognitive remediation training is an example of training to improve cognition. This involves targeting specific aspects of cognition such as working memory training, where you have to recall the last five people you spoke with. Cognitive remediation is still in its early stages of development, but some online tools are starting to emerge and be used by researchers and therapists. Some tools include HappyNeuron (US$99 for therapists to use with unlimited patients), CogSMART (free), and RehaCom (£80 for forty-five hours of use).

Self-care and self-development programs

You can undertake training that supports your treatment program. For example, you might enrol in mindfulness training, stress reduction training, understanding depression and anxiety and women's well-being and empowerment. You may enrol in self-care programs such as cooking, budgeting, gardening and blogging or learn new skills such as car maintenance and using social media.

You may also take the opportunity to enrol in self-development programs such as an IT course, a photography course, learning a foreign language, a first-aid course and learning a musical instrument.

Educating yourself about mental health

You should also keep learning about your mental health and how to improve it. Evidence-based practice is an essential element in how you see treatment. Make sure there is good research behind a practice. Even if a professional suggests a treatment plan or new medication, ask them for the evidence behind the treatment. Read more from quality sources such as open-access Cochrane reviews (a way to bring together a lot of reputable research into one article) or research done by consumers for consumers.

Lived experience vignette — Mark's observations on recovery

For me, recovery is mostly about preventing relapses or reducing their impact if they do happen. This involves taking the right medication, seeing a psychologist and a psychiatrist, dieting and exercising. I'm not so good at the dieting and exercise part, but these are very important because psychosis often leads to poor physical health, and exercise can actually improve your mental health. Recovery for me also involves finding a new career given that the stressors of my past careers – being a marketing manager and then academic – might negatively affect my mood or cause further psychotic episodes. Recovery is also about dealing with the traumatic memories of my past persecutory delusions.

Lived experience vignette — Jamie's observations on recovery

I think one of the biggest problems is like it is changing definitely, but one of the biggest problems is that we don't talk enough about psychosis, and there's a lot of people who can't make meaning out of it, and then they feel that it's not normal and that there's something wrong with them, which makes them fear the voices more, which makes the voices then turn very nasty.

Lived experience vignette — Orbit's observations on recovery

I was adopted and have had a difficult life since. I truly believe that I am the child of a recent past prime minister. There are many facts that have led to this belief. People think it's a delusion, but I have held this belief for many years, even while I was heavily medicated. I don't like labels, but some people call me 'genderqueer', but I wear feminine clothing mostly. I have been scheduled a few times, but now my life is relatively stable, having just got a place to stay through a Sydney charity after twenty years on the streets. I feel like I have brain damage, which makes doing things very hard, but I still have hope things will get better for me. Luckily, I have one of the top psychiatrists in Australia, and I don't have to go to a public hospital because he is private. I told all this to Mark, and he could really empathise. I've let him use this brief story but without my real name and with a few facts changed.

Support persons' role

Adjusting to the new reality

Support persons need to understand that recovery does not mean that everything will 'go back to normal'. This may be the case, but more often, there are lasting physical and psychological effects from psychosis-related disorders. Supporters need to understand that even if there is no disorder diagnosed, the trauma of psychosis can last a lifetime. The role of the supporter is to provide encouragement and foster hope.

The support person's role does include being aware of early warning signs of a relapse; however, it is difficult to keep this in perspective as you and the person you support may still be recovering from the experience of the previous episode. The anxiety may be compounded if the person has been recently discharged from hospital, and as a support person, you are feeling the responsibility is now on you. You need to discuss this together and give space when it is asked for. You may like to get permission from the person you care for to talk to their medical practitioners. You don't need to know everything that goes on in their sessions but should be able to report unusual behaviour, being careful not to lose the trust of the person you care for.

At the recovery and renewal stages, you may need to resist your temptation to constantly question new behaviours. These may not be a sign of relapse but instead a sign of learning from past experiences and changing past behaviour. Examples of the fine distinction between behaviour indicating illness and behaviour indicating recovery include the following:

- Becoming more active with multiple work or charity projects. This may be a sign of mania for people with bipolar, but if stress from new projects is well-managed, it may be a healthy part of recovery.
- Being really happy can also seem like mania for people with bipolar I. If there is a clear source of happiness though, it could be very normal.
- Changing religions or forming new spiritual beliefs. This could be the result of delusions or could be a rational reaction to difficult

circumstances. Make sure they are not being taken advantage of by religious groups but respect new beliefs.

- Severing old relationships may be a sign of paranoia, social isolation or persecutory delusions, but if those relationships were harmful to mental health, they may need to be severed as part of recovery.
- Setting new very bold goals may be a sign of grandiose delusions but, if they are not too extreme, may be the result of a strong desire for self-improvement or for helping others.
- Noticing strange coincidences and trying to interpret the connections between things may be a sign of delusions of reference. However, there may be undeniable evidence of the connections or new beliefs in luck or superstitions that many people with no history of psychosis also believe.

If you find the new behaviour really doesn't fit with your previous perceptions of the person you support, you might still like to consult a medical professional for their advice. The professional will most likely then want to see the person you support to make their own assessment, balancing out all available evidence. Try not to allow this professional to use your anecdotes as the main grounds for involuntary treatment as you and they may have misinterpreted things or failed to see the full picture.

Encouraging counselling

Having recently experienced a psychotic episode, the person you support is likely to be self-absorbed – just trying to survive – and still illness focused. They have a lot to cope with. They may be the following:

- Anxious about relapsing
- Traumatised by the diagnosis they've been labelled with
- Traumatised by the symptoms they've suffered from their illness
- Traumatised by the experience of being hospitalised for a mental illness and the treatment associated with it
- Profoundly changed by their illness, the impact of the illness and the medication they're taking
- Grieving so many losses – the changes in their identity and the loss of some friends, relatives, partners, work
- Experiencing stigma as a result of their label and behaviour etc

- Unable to resume their former jobs and wondering where to go from here
- Self-absorbed, just trying to cope with 'normal' activities of daily living

They need lots of support to be able to cope with all this. They need a treatment plan that includes professional support that gives opportunities for the person to work through some of these areas. As a support person, you can listen and comfort but encourage them to seek professional help, such as seeing a psychologist or counsellor, joining an outpatient program with the community mental health team or private hospital, joining online forums etc.

Moving forwards

Encourage the person you support to plan self-care activities focusing on re-establishing their lives as part of their treatment plan. It may be helpful to think in the CHIME framework of connectedness, hope, identity, meaning and empowerment. Encourage conversations in this framework, support the person you care for with self-care activities and recognise and celebrate successes. Encourage activities that you would normally do together, such as going to a café or the cinema, going shopping together, cooking a meal together, taking a walk together, going on an outing together and visiting friends together.

Tread carefully to maintain communication and trust

After all that you've been through together, there are challenges in communicating and maintaining trust. Don't try to do too much. Try to let the person you support take the lead. Think about what your role is as a support person. You are not there to give advice or treatment or tell them what to do. You are essentially there to listen, encourage and give positive support. Your best option is to try to do easy activities together that you know they enjoy. This helps to make you and the person you support feel a little better, more connected and more 'normal.'

Supporter vignette — A mum's experience of hospitalisation and recovery

Scheduled into an acute mental health ward. Staff in central – glass fishbowl. Patients circling around them outside the bowl, largely left to their own devices and asking to see their doctor. Wanting out. What do you have to do to be discharged? Speak to patients who know the ropes. You need to be observed by staff to be acting normal, such as by engaging with others, participating in any activities, using the treadmill if there is one. Medication is the only answer. Just get the meds stabilised. Try an overnight at home. If that goes OK, you're out.

Psychiatrist focused on 'diagnosis'. This determines medications. Disagreement about diagnosis – bipolar or schizoaffective? Either way, the problem for Mark is violent, rapid-onset mood swings between mania and depression. How do you medicate for this?

Massive doses of a range of drugs – antipsychotics, mood stabilisers, antidepressants. They take time to kick in, time to regulate dosage. Side effects, interactions, warnings. Tremor, weight gain, drowsiness, restlessness, memory loss. Damage to liver. Damage to thyroid. Is it the illness or the medication?

Meds stabilised. Acting 'normal'. Nine days. Night at home. Family meeting with doctor after return from night out. All of us still in shock from whole episode. Scared that it's too early. But out, it is. Not sleeping. Struggling. Frenzied activity. Just escort him by day and manage with Ray by night. So angry with us. Mad about my driving. Gets out while car is moving. Finally presents at hospital emergency at midnight with a cold. Re-admitted to psych ward. Repeat. Out again.

This is our new reality. This is not a once-off episode. Still trying to work out the diagnosis and medication and manage the ups and downs. Fear. Any change makes us nervous. Is this an early warning? Will it get worse? Not sleeping is our biggest risk. This is perhaps our major indicator that all is not well and needs to be acted on quickly.

A huge adjustment for Mark. He has an illness that he will need to live with for his whole life. He is a different person. The illness, the experience of the illness and the medication all affect him profoundly – physically, psychologically, socially and cognitively. He has a different personality. He is quiet, withdrawn – head down, doesn't initiate conversation, concrete thinking. There doesn't appear to be much joy in his life. He has gained weight. He finds it difficult to get out of bed or do any activities. He finds it difficult to concentrate. He is restless. He hasn't read a book.

He tries. He enjoys music. He sees his friends. He gardens. He enjoys Ray's company. I like that they are close and laugh together. They go to shows. Mark applies for jobs. He continues some online teaching. He tries full-time work, but he can't manage it yet. Work was so important to him and so much the focus of his life. He realises that, at least for the time being, he cannot do what he did previously. He has to find a new job. What job should that be? He gets knock-backs. It is tough.

We are mourning the loss of the old Mark and getting to know the new Mark. It is not bad – just different.

Supporter vignette — A partner's experience of recovery

While Mark was in hospital, the doctors and nurses failed to give me adequate information about how to help him and how to prepare for discharge. I had to persistently call them and look around the ward for information. I had to make sure we had more stable accommodation and tried to reduce some of the stressors that led up to his psychotic break, but this took time. Without much notice, Mark was given overnight leave, but he was not ready for it, and we had to take him back. A week later, he was discharged, which was a mistake. He was sedated and did not have much emotion, but then a few weeks after discharge, he manically started to create a new business and worked on his legal case against the university. He showed a few signs of relapse or perhaps a continuation of the initial episode, like texting and emailing weird things and reacting in panic when contacted by his manager and a colleague. He needed another hospitalisation, and this time, he called the ambulance himself.

After this second admission, recovery was very slow. He was clearly depressed and didn't eat much. He also had breakthrough psychotic symptoms about mundane things like our blanket and our cat. I told his psychiatrist about this as he couldn't recognise it as unusual, and his medication was changed. He gained a lot of weight from the antipsychotic medication he was put on and was told he might have schizophrenia. We did some mindfulness practice, which helped momentarily. We tried to get him to a private hospital, but this was not possible when he was acutely unwell.

I arranged his medical certificates and handled most of his compensation claim and then his temporary incapacity claim, which is like income protection. His compensation claim was eventually denied, and the whole process was traumatic for everyone. The basis of the denial was that he was fine now and that the past episode was irrelevant. An appeal was possible but would have aggravated Mark's illness, so we left it. He was not fine; he was deeply depressed for six months and then hospitalised for psychosis again but this time in a private hospital. He found a job while in hospital, which gave him a sense of purpose, but became depressed again and struggled to work full-time. He changed meds a few times and got better with one change, but it set his mood off balance, leading to mania, psychosis and another hospitalisation. Recovery for him so far has been about reducing the severity of each relapse, keeping occupied despite depression, maintaining connections with friends, writing, attending group therapy and going into private hospital as soon as early warning signs appear.

Renewal

Recovery is the dominant paradigm in care for people after a psychotic episode. Recovery suggests making progress in trying to regain what you had before your first episode. This may not be *fully* possible and might not even be desirable. Instead, your aim after you have stabilised can be renewal – creating a new self that has learned from the experience of psychosis. It is a focus on the whole person – on re-establishing your life and re-inventing yourself where needed. The ultimate goal is the WHO definition of mental health, which is achieving 'a state of well-being in which every individual realises his or her own potential, can cope with the normal stresses of life, can work productively and fruitfully and is able to make a contribution to her or his community'.

Renewal is a personal journey of discovery that includes new learning on how to live life well. It is up to you to take the reins and work out what you want your life to look like.

To do this, you need a robust team of health professionals who can help facilitate your journey to wellness. This team needs to be client centred, focused, driven and made up of team members with whom you have an ongoing relationship who are positive, supportive, hopeful and available and who know your history and needs, and the whole team works with you to help you identify and achieve your goals to lead a full and productive life. Ideally, this whole service would be provided by the community mental health team. The key is that you need to take control. You need to get this team whatever way you can. You may need assistance from your supporters to advocate for you to help you achieve this.

The team needs to include the following:

- A GP, who manages the coordination of the medical aspects of your condition as well as directs you to other services as appropriate

and supports you to identify your priorities, goals, barriers and the professionals who can help you on your journey
- A psychiatrist, who manages your medication and therapy
- A psychologist, who helps you plan your renewal program, identify and deal with anything that's getting in the way of your recovery and supports you to implement the program
- Other health professionals in line with your goals

The other critical component is a strong support group who are positive, supportive and hopeful and listen to you. They support you on your journey. They advocate for you if you request it. They recognise and celebrate your achievements with you. They support you through setbacks. They support your choices.

Life with a complex mental health condition is challenging. Recurring episodes and hospital admissions are associated with total powerlessness and no control. A lifetime on medication reduces control and compounds powerlessness because of frequent overmedication and the side effects of medications. The mental health system is totally inadequate to meet the needs of people with episodes of psychosis. They frequently cannot access the services they need. They may not be able to access services at all. Services are fragmented and uncoordinated. It is a tough journey. The path to renewal involves turning the bad things in your life into good things. This can be done in many ways, such as the following:

- Using your experience of psychosis to help others with similar symptoms
- Pursuing goals you developed during grandiose delusions – or at least more realistic versions of them
- Facing past trauma and getting it treated properly
- Eliminating or reducing stressful situations
- Entering a new career that better fits your values

Renewal is about change. Change is challenging. Focus on your strengths and values. Be realistic and practical. Take small steps. Celebrate your successes. Look back at every day and find something positive and hopeful in what you've done each day. Don't beat yourself up about setbacks. Try something different. Try to learn from your setbacks.

We hope that this guide will demystify psychosis and help you on your journey. We invite you to share your journey with us on madnarratives. com.au.

Rise like a phoenix

Out of the ashes of psychosis, you will eventually be able to become someone new, someone strong. Going through persecutory delusions and paranoia is a particularly awful experience, and you are blessed if your psychosis only includes grandiosity. However, these experiences teach you to better cope with fear, difficult situations and intense negativity. You will also likely develop a new appreciation for those who support you and gain a greater respect for the power of your mind.

After psychosis or any extremely troubling experience, you may go through 'post-traumatic growth'. This may take years to occur, but if it does, it involves becoming wiser, more compassionate and stronger because of traumatic experiences. The trauma may not go away, as is suggested by the term *recovery*, but there may be new qualities you develop because of the trauma as you go through a 'renewal'.

Activity: Glass half-full

List all the positive things to come out of your experiences with psychosis. This could include new knowledge/skills and new or stronger relationships.

Are you normal?

During the recovery and renewal stages, people may question your behaviour and ask themselves or ask you directly whether you are becoming delusional again. You may also start to question your own thoughts and wonder whether you are experiencing breakthrough psychotic symptoms. This may happen when you are thinking certain types of thoughts, such as considering new religious or spiritual beliefs, setting ambitious goals or making assumptions about what certain people think of you.

The important thing is to keep thinking grand and deep thoughts. Don't let the fear of a potential psychotic break silence your intelligence and wisdom. Drawing on thoughts from when you were psychotic will seem dangerous to you and even more so to those who were with you during psychosis, but there might be some gems there that your mind constructs when making new connections with old knowledge. The way to ensure you are not experiencing breakthrough psychotic symptoms is to apply the scientific method to your thinking (known as critical thinking). This can be done through the following:

1. Posing your initial thoughts as questions rather than facts
2. Gathering information from experts on the topic and looking for opinions and facts that answer your question in opposing ways
3. If you don't have facts for something, thinking about the probability for each alternate explanation for why something is the way it is
4. Accepting that you may not ever find total truth about a matter and being prepared to listen to new evidence that comes in to better answer your question

Psychosis may actually help you get a better understanding of what is real and what humans have made up in their heads. Just as you may have hallucinated or generated a false belief with a delusion, you can start to recognise how some things we accept as true are actually not based on hard evidence.

Fighting stigma

People with mental health conditions have to put up with not only the illness associated with the condition but also the burden of the stigma associated with mental health conditions. In the words of Sydney actor Annalise Braakensiek, who talked openly about her struggles with mental health, 'mental health has so many misconceptions, criticism, misunderstandings and false judgements still'.

Stigma is when someone views you in a negative way. There are three components to stigma. They are the following:

- **Ignorance** or lack of knowledge about mental health conditions.
- **Prejudice or negative attitudes**. You may, for example, be called names like psycho, loony, nutter, freak or retard or told to 'just get over it' or 'pull yourself together'. You may feel ashamed for something that is out of your control. Negative attitudes may, in fact, be a barrier to seeking treatment for mental health conditions.
- **Discrimination**, which may involve excluding or avoiding people with mental health conditions. People may, for example, avoid you because they feel you are out of control and they are a little scared by your behaviour. You may even judge yourself and isolate yourself from others or avoid talking about your condition.

Stigma about psychosis often relates to a misunderstanding of what psychosis is and a false assumption that psychosis is permanent. There has been much progress destigmatising anxiety and depression, but psychosis still has a long way to go.

Some of the harmful effects of stigma may include the following:

- Losing belief in yourself and giving up
- Reluctance to seek help or treatment
- Feeling that you're not understood by family, friends, co-workers etc
- Being harassed or bullied
- Being victimised
- Being isolated and not having opportunities for school or social activities
- Being discriminated against in regard to areas including jobs and housing
- Lack of understanding by family, friends, co-workers or others

- Fewer opportunities for work, school or social activities or trouble finding housing
- Health insurance that doesn't adequately cover treatment of your mental health condition

No matter what your role is in the mental health area, you can make a difference by talking openly about mental health, not letting people get away with negative comments, showing compassion for others and setting an example. Mental health conditions are illnesses. No matter what others say, an illness is no one's fault. Blame the illness, not the person, for bad things that have happened.

As a person with a mental health condition, you can fight against stigma in a number of ways. However, it is also important that you are mindful about when and how you do this. When you recognise stigma, you should first consider your own position. Aspects that you may need to bear in mind in regard to stigma include the following:

- Am I letting my own fear of being labelled with a mental health condition stop me from seeking help or getting treatment? Treatment helps by identifying what's wrong and reducing symptoms that may be interfering with your work and personal life.
- Is the 'stigma' real or part of my illness?
- Is it within my interest to stand up to the 'stigma'? For example, it may be detrimental to disclose a mental health condition during an initial interview for a job.
- Could there be detrimental consequences to my disclosure of my mental health condition?
- Am I strong enough at the moment to be able to discuss my condition with others?

Remember that other people's judgements almost always stem from a lack of understanding rather than information based on facts. Accepting your condition, recognising what you need to do to treat it, seeking support and helping educate others can make a big difference.

As a person with a mental health condition or as a carer, friend or relative, you can stand up against stigma when you feel strong enough. You can do this by doing the following:

- Educating yourself about mental health so you can talk sensibly and rationally to others.
- Fighting against ignorance by talking openly about your experience with mental health to help educate yourself and others.
- Choosing empowerment over shame by not allowing others to dictate how you feel.
- Sharing your story.
- Explaining that mental health conditions are illnesses, including reminding people that they wouldn't make fun of someone with cancer or a heart condition or diabetes.
- Speaking out against stigma that you see on TV, movies or social media.
- Standing up against prejudice and discrimination by reminding people that their language matters.
- Showing compassion for others with mental health conditions by empathising with them.
- Connecting with others who have similar conditions who can help you gain self-esteem and overcome destructive self-judgement.

Lived experience vignette — Mark's observations on renewal

I recently had another major episode of psychosis and handled it worse than the previous ones. At the most severe point, I was in hospital and thought I was being pursued into my room by violent criminals out to kill me. I treated my carers and other family abhorrently.

As such, I don't consider myself in the renewal or even recovery phase. I am, however, very glad to have forged many new connections in hospital and outpatient clinics. I have learned a great deal about overcoming adversity from those around me. I have seen many homeless people with experience of psychosis to deal with their condition and find stable housing. Some take a few days to overcome an acute and transient episode. Others take weeks, months or years. Relapse feels like a huge setback, but there is always hope that I will find a new and different path that makes a contribution to society.

Hearing voices

Many people with chronic psychosis live with constant voices in their head. Medication is ineffective in eliminating voices in over 25 per cent of cases (De Jager and Rhodes, 2013). If you live with voices, recovery may be about quieting them, learning not to act on the voices and learning to pay attention to situations even when voices are distracting you.

The most concerning voices are those that are 'command hallucinations', which tell you to harm yourself or others. Command hallucinations quickly need to be dispelled with medication, argued against logically if possible, drowned out with music or the other strategies listed in the Therapy section.

There are Hearing Voices Networks in most states that are based on a global movement which sees voice hearing as not always an indicator of psychosis. The UK-based Hearing Voices Network (2018) defines recovery as 'living the life you choose, not the life others choose for you'. The book *Living with Voices: 50 Stories of Recovery* is a good resource for finding first-hand stories of hearing voices. In this book, hearing voices is not seen as a sign of madness but instead a reaction to serious problems in life. Alternative perspectives like this may help you reframe how you think about your voice hearing, but be careful not to go off your medication because you attribute voices to trauma rather than psychosis. The Hearing Voices movement can be reassuring and reduce stigma, but their methods are not backed by strong evidence (Corstens et al, 2014).

Antipsychiatry movement

Just as the Hearing Voices movement questions whether voice hearing is a result of psychosis, the antipsychiatry movement questions whether the medical model of psychosis is accurate. Some people find elements of the antipsychiatry movement useful in their recovery because they are angry about the harm inflicted on them by involuntary treatment, side effects and unhelpful therapists. If you are morbidly obese because of medication, traumatised from police scheduling you and being restrained and injected or have involuntary body movements that even persist after ceasing medication (known as Tardive dyskinesia), you have every right to be angry.

Ronald D. Laing was central to antipsychiatry. He wrote particularly about schizophrenia and claimed it was 'a sane reaction to an insane world' and that the mental hospital was no place to treat schizophrenia (*New York Times*, 1989). A person with schizophrenia was seen as the scapegoat of a dysfunctional family, and Laing believed 'without exception the experience and behaviour that gets labelled as schizophrenia is a special strategy that the patient invents to live with an unliveable situation' (Howe, 1991).

Turning to antipsychiatry might not be the answer though. Ruffalo (2017) makes the argument that 'just as coercive psychiatrists deprive patients of their constitutional protections under the guise of medical treatment, the antipsychiatrists insist that certain treatments or psychiatry altogether must be banned in the name of protecting people from harm'. So advocacy for greater rights for those treated involuntarily is a positive thing and shouldn't turn into an outright hate for all psychiatric treatment. Psychiatric hospitals and community treatment save the lives of many, even though for a minority, they feel like the cause is of a sense that your mental health is in ruins. The level of control psychiatry exerts on individuals and on society is clearly significant (Foucault, 1965), but your advocacy can help rectify some of the power imbalance.

Mad Pride

Normality may not be your goal. Instead, you may start to enjoy being outside the norm. The Mad Pride movement embraces the usually derogatory word *mad* and campaigns in a similar way to gay pride. The movement has died out somewhat, but there are still occasional Mad Pride concerts in Australia. Like the gay pride movement, Mad Pride is a celebration rooted in a protest.

Less grand gestures of pride may be more appropriate for your renewal. The idea of 'coming out' with a mental illness like LGBTI people who come out of the closet can help reduce stigma. This includes self-stigma because you learn to live your life openly and honestly and connect with others who have also come out with mental illness.

There are specific interventions to help you learn to come out proud. These are often led by peers. In these sessions or independently, you should consider '(a) risks and benefits of secrecy and disclosure in different settings; (b) levels of disclosure, between the extremes of social withdrawal/secrecy and broadcasting one's experience with mental illness; and (c) on helpful ways to tell one's story with mental illness, again in different settings' (Rüsch et al, 2014). Deciding who to disclose to, what to tell them and how to explain it is important at each stage of your journey, from the first episode of psychosis to renewal. Some of the decisions may have already been made for you as people find out about your ill health through interacting with you while you were unwell or hearing gossip. Your path to renewal should involve setting the record straight with as many of these people as you can or forgetting those who misunderstood you and your illness.

Resources

Getting help in an emergency

If you or someone you are with is in immediate danger, call 000 and ask for the police. The police will estimate the risk of violence when they arrive at the premises. Police are generally well-trained to help get the person to the best possible treatment. It can be frightening when the police arrive. However, there is no need to be afraid if police are involved in taking you to hospital. If the person has a weapon or is threatening others, the police may need to take appropriate action. In this case, it is important for the caller to the police to stress that the person has a mental health condition and just needs to be escorted to hospital.

State and territory government mental health crisis lines

Mental health crisis lines are another option in an emergency situation, particularly when the person may be a threat to themselves and/or others. In this case, they may respond to your call by coming to you accompanied by police officers.

ACT Mental Health Triage Service 1800 629 354	**NSW Mental Health Help Line** 1800 011 511
Northern Territory Crisis Assessment and Telephone Triage and Liaison Service 1800 682 288	**Queensland Health Advice** 13 HEALTH (13 43 25 84)
South Australia Assessment and Crisis Intervention Service 131 465	**Tasmania Mental Health Services Helpline** 1800 332 388
Victoria SuicideLine 1300 651 251	**Western Australia Mental Health Emergency Response Line** 1300 555 788

Free telephone support

If you or someone you are with is in immediate danger, you must call 000.	
Lifeline Australia 13 11 14 24 hour crisis support including online chat	**SANE Helpline** 1800 187 263 Weekdays 10am-10pm AEST
One Door 1800 843 539 Weekdays 9am-5pm AEST	**Wellways** 1300 111 400 Weekdays 9am-9pm AEST
Suicide Call Back Service 1300 659 467 24 hour crisis support including online chat	**Beyond Blue** 1300 22 4636 24 hour support for depression and anxiety
MensLine Australia 1300 78 99 78 24 hour crisis support for Men	**Kids Helpline** 1800 55 1800 24 hour support for young people aged 5-25
GriefLine 1300 845 745 Support for grief 12pm-3am AEST	**1800RESPECT** 1800 737 732 24 hour support for abuse or sexual assault
Q Life 1800 184 527 Support for LGBTI people 3pm-Midnight	**The Butterfly Foundation** 1800 33 4673 Support for eating disorders 8-12am AEST
Healthdirect 1800 022 222 Support from a registered nurse or GP	**Grow** 1800 558 268 Groups that meet for 2hrs on mental health
Relationships Australia 1300 364 277 Relationship support services	**Blue Knot Foundation Helpline** 1300 657 380 Support for complex trauma
Family Drug Support 1300 368 186 24 hour support for carers of drug users	**Carers Australia** 1800 242 636 9am-5pm weekday support for carers
PANDA 1300 726 306 Perinatal support weekdays 9am-7:30pm AEST	**Veterans and Veterans Families Counselling Service (VVCS)** 1800 011 046 24 hour support for vets and their families

Online Australian resources

Psychosis Australia Trust Resources on psychosis psychosisaustralia.com.au	**SANE Australia** Forums and facts on complex mental health sane.org
Head to Health Directory of mental health resources headtohealth.gov.au	**Australian Psychology Society** Resources and directory of psychologists psychology.org.au

ReachOut Forums and articles for young people au.reachout.com	eheadspace Online support for people aged 12–25 eheadspace.org.au
Beyond Blue Anxiety and depression resources beyondblue.org.au	Black Dog Institute Information on mood disorders blackdoginstitute.org.au
mindhealthconnect Online programs and resources mindhealthconnect.org.au	Mental Health First Aid A course in recognising mental illness mhfa.com.au
Centre for Corporate Health Resources for workplaces cfch.com.au	Heads Up More resources for workplaces headsup.org.au
R U OK? Suicide prevention movement ruok.org.au	Children of Parents with a Mental Illness Resources for your children copmi.net.au
Mental Health Australia Resources for consumers and carers mhaustralia.org	MindSpot Clinic Online treatment for anxiety and depression mindspot.org.au
This is My Reality Australian mental health stories and poems thisismyreality.com.au	Schizophrenia Fellowship Blog on schizophrenia schizophrenia.org.au
Orygen Resources for youth mental health orygen.org.au	NeuRA Research resources including a blog neura.edu.au
Mind Australia Resources to support individuals recover in the community www.mindaustralia.org.au	

Notable apps

Black Dog Institute, Snapshot Free Helps monitor well-being	How Are You Going? Mind Australia Free Helps monitor well-being	Mindshift Free Strategies to help control stress and worry
Twenty-Four Hours a Day $8.49 Meditation for addiction iPhone and Android	Quit That! Free or paid upgrades Reduces addiction iPhone	Sobriety Counter Free with ads or upgrades Tracks multiple addictions Android
eMoods Free Bipolar mood tracker iPhone and Android	iMoodJournal $4.49 Mood tracker iPhone and Android	Daylio Free with ads or upgrades Journal and mood tracker iPhone and Android

MoodKit $7.99 Mood improvement tools iPhone	CBT Thought Record Diary Free iPhone and Android	MoodMission Free but requires surveys Help with mood and anxiety iPhone and Android
Breathe2Relax Free Stress management iPhone and Android	BeyondNow Suicide Safety Free Suicide prevention iPhone, Android and web	Calm Harm Free Manages self-harm iPhone and Android
Smiling Mind Free Meditation and mindfulness iPhone and Android	Headspace US$13/month Simplifies meditation iPhone and Android	Calm US$13/month Meditation and mindfulness iPhone and Android
FoodSwitch Free Swipe bar code for healthier food options	Mindbody Free Helps locate healthy mind and body activities	Lumosity Free Fun brain games
Stop, Breathe and Think Free Guided meditation and mindful reflection	Balanced Free Reminds you to lead a balanced life	Beyond Blue, Check-in Free Helps you have conversations about mental health

Notable books about psychosis

A Mother's Climb Out Of Darkness Jennifer H. Moyer Memoir about postpartum psychosis	Broken Open Craig Hamilton Australian memoir including grandiose delusions from bipolar
Demons in the Age of Light Whitney Robinson Memoir of psychosis and recovery	Diagnosis: Psychosis Olivia Russo True story of stress-induced psychosis
Eating Smoke Chris Thrall A story of ice psychosis and Hong Kong triads	Experiencing Psychosis: Personal and Professional Perspectives Jim Geekie et al First-person accounts of psychosis
Fairy Tales in Reality Margo Orum Australian book featuring psychosis from bipolar	In Two Minds Gordon Parker Australian novel by a psychiatry professor, includes psychosis from bipolar
Lowboy John Wray Story of a young person with schizophrenia	Madness Explained: Psychosis and Human Nature Richard P. Bentall Radical perspective on psychosis

My Punished Mind David C. Boyles Memoir of life with schizoaffective disorder	*No One Cares About Crazy People* Ron Powers U.S. memoir from a father of two men with schizophrenia and history of mental illness
Psychosis in Childhood and Adolescence James B. McCarthy Research-based book for early psychosis	*Psychosis: Stories of Recovery and Hope* Jane Fradgley et al Information and UK narratives about psychosis
Rethinking Madness Paris Williams Resources and alternative theories on psychosis	*Tell Me I'm Here* Anne Deveson Australian memoir of a mother's perspective on her son who has schizophrenia
The Canary: A Journey Through Psychosis Jeff Malderez Story of a young man with psychosis	*The Day the Voices Stopped* Ken Steele and Claire Berman Story of recovery from schizophrenia
The First Episode of Psychosis: A Guide for Patients and Their Families Michael T. Compton	*Understanding Psychosis and Schizophrenia* Anne Cooke Guide from the British Psychological Society

Notable movies about psychosis

There are a lot of movies about psychopaths but not many about psychosis. With movies – or indeed any medium about mental health – you need to be careful not to let the stories of illness re-traumatise you or reinforce false myths about psychosis. Stop the movie or call a support line if you are triggered by any themes.

The Snake Pit (1948) About a woman who appears to have schizophrenia and her successful recovery	*Lilith* (1964) A story of a woman in a private mental hospital who has lost touch with reality
The Fisher King (1991) A story of delusions and hallucinations induced by violent trauma	*Benny and Joon* (1993) A love story involving a woman who experienced hallucinations
Clean, Shaven (1993) Violent but insightful movie on a man with schizophrenia	*Angel Baby* (1995) Australian love story about two people with schizophrenia
Pi (1998) A movie on a highly paranoid mathematician	*Requiem for a Dream* (2000) A movie on drug addiction, including an instance of drug-induced psychosis
A Beautiful Mind (2001) True story of John Nash, the mathematician with schizophrenia	*Revolution #9* (2001) Story of a fairly normal man with delusions and paranoia who is hospitalised

Donnie Darko (2001)	*The White Sound* (2001)
Movie about a hallucination that encourages a man to commit crimes	German film about magic mushrooms and schizophrenia
Reprise (2006)	*The Soloist* (2009)
A story of two writers; one experiences psychosis and is hospitalised	Story of a gifted musician with schizophrenia
Voices (2013)	*Brain on Fire* (2016)
U.S. documentary on three people with psychosis	True story of an rare illness causing psychosis symptoms

Notable TV shows about psychosis

There are not many TV shows with the central theme of psychosis, but the following list involves shows with at least one character who experiences hallucinations, delusions or related mental health conditions. Like the movies on psychosis, television does not often get these issues right.

Bedlam	*Eli Stone*
A UK documentary currently available on YouTube with an episode on psychosis	Two-season series about a lawyer who has hallucinations
Homeland	*Legion*
Series about the CIA, with Claire Danes playing a bipolar agent with delusions	Marvel series about a mutant diagnosed with schizophrenia
Mental	*Mr Robot*
Single-season 2009 show on a psychiatrist treating psychosis and other conditions	About a vigilante hacker with psychosis
Orange Is the New Black	*Perception*
Not about mental health, but two characters experience psychosis	Crime series about a neuropsychiatrist with hallucinations from schizophrenia
Shameless	*United States of Tara*
Includes the character Ian, who has bipolar and experiences psychosis with mania	Not about psychosis but about the condition often confused with schizophrenia – dissociative identity disorder

Afterword

To address each of the areas of your life that may be impacted by psychosis, our goal with treatment is to achieve a state of well-being by eliminating, reducing or living well despite symptoms, preventing or minimising the impact of relapses, living life well and dealing with challenges as they arise to lead a productive and enjoyable life that includes making a contribution to your community if that's your goal.

To achieve this, the treatment plan takes a holistic wellness approach to health by identifying how psychosis impacts each aspect of your life – including the physical, psychological and social aspects of your life – and the impact of each area on yourself, your activities of daily life, your interactions with others, your studies, your work and other activities.

This is particularly important for those of us who've had a psychotic episode. We need to take control of our lives and do everything in our power to make a full recovery wherever possible and create the best possible situation to prevent another episode. This includes working on physical, psychological and social well-being relevant to your own journey.

We can also learn to live with psychotic symptoms and minimise our use of medication. This needs to be done in consultation with medical professionals and support people, but the voice of consumers is the most important, and our wishes when we are well must be respected.

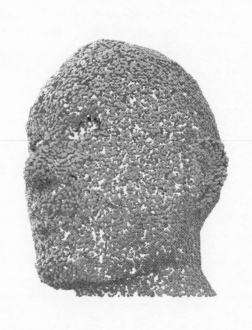

Index

P

Parkinson's disease 15-16
Perinatal Anxiety & Depression
     Australia (PANDA) 15
pre-psychosis treatment 20
privacy 59
Psychoeducation 68-9
psychosis:
  acute 45, 53
  drug-induced 12
  postnatal 13-15

R

recovery ix-xi, 13, 19, 24, 41, 48, 50,
    59, 67-8, 73-4, 79-82, 84-5, 89,
    93, 113

S

SANE Australia v, ix-x, 110
schizoaffective 49-50, 63
schizophrenia ix, 7, 43, 46, 48-9,
    62-4, 113
schizotypal disorder 8
self-care 23, 38, 40, 57, 66, 80, 90
self-soothing 24, 66
setbacks 85
social media 26, 28-9, 50-1
stress ix, 9, 20, 26-8, 35, 41, 71
stroke 15-16, 18, 42-3

suicide 6, 43, 82

T

therapy 6, 10, 37, 40, 56-7, 62, 66-7,
    70-2, 74
  art 71
  befriending 68, 70-1
  family 71
  music 68, 71
trauma 67
treatment plan 23-4, 31, 36-7, 48-9,
    53, 57, 67, 73, 85-6
tribunals 72-3

U

University of Queensland 43
urge surfing 41
U.S. National Institute of Mental
    Health 63

W

Weight Watchers Australia 42
well-being 25, 36-7, 40, 42, 80-2,
    84-6
wellness 35, 79, 81, 84-5
World Health Organisation
    (WHO) 80